ADDICTIVE
THINKING

ÁDDICTIVE
THINKING,

Understanding Self-Deception

Abraham J. Twerski, M.D.

1817

A Harper/Hazelden Book
Harper & Row, Publishers, San Francisco
New York, Grand Rapids, Philadelphia, St. Louis
London, Singapore, Sydney, Tokyo, Toronto

FIRST HARPER & ROW EDITION PUBLISHED IN 1990.

Library of Congress Cataloging-in-Publication Data

Twerski, Abraham J.
    Addictive thinking : understanding self-deception / Abraham Twerski. — 1st Harper & Row ed.
        p.   cm.
    "A Harper/Hazelden book."
    ISBN 0-06-255397-6
    1. Compulsive behavior.   2. Self-deception.   I. Title.
RC533.T9   1990
616.85′227—dc20   89-84785
                                                         CIP

90 91 92 93 94   MAPLE   10 9 8 7 6 5 4 3 2 1

This edition is printed on acid-free paper that meets the American National Standards Institute Z39.48 Standard.

CONTENTS

FOREWORD

Addiction and codependency can manifest themselves in many forms. The addict is not always aware of the subtle development of addiction until he or she becomes addicted. If the addict does not want to change or stop the addiction, he or she must develop a strong denial system.

The same is true for those who live with and love an addict. They are negatively affected by the addict's addiction, and this can lead them to the development of codependent behaviors. Codependency develops much like addiction: it depends on denial and comes on a person subtly.

Addiction and codependency share one more characteristic. They both involve very complicated and contradictory thinking patterns. These thinking patterns, which are present in most addicts and codependents, have been identified by Dr. Twerski as addictologia. How many times, when we are trying to understand addicts or codependents, have we asked ourselves, *What in the world are they thinking?*

The lives of addicts and codependents are full of many contradictions in behaviors and explanations. Addicts claim they need no one, but then ask you to cover up for their behaviors. Codependents claim they are not affected by the addiction of another, but then proceed to alter their behaviors to accommodate the addict. How could these behavioral patterns not only emerge, but also appear to be "normal" or "logical" to the addict or codependent?

The answer can be found by discovering how the addict or the codependent thinks, especially how he or she thinks about addiction. In other words, the way in which people think can contribute not only to the development of addiction or codependency, but can also create barriers to recovery.

The discovery of addictive thinking in addicts and codependents begins to offer insight into the many paradoxes of addiction. Addictive thinking leads many people to the conclusion that they are engaging in perfectly logical behavior. In fact, they are often so convinced that their behaviors are justified that, in treatment, they may convincingly rationalize their behaviors to themselves and the therapist. Addictive thinking can be contagious, and the therapist must be careful not to become infected.

Some of the paradoxes of addictive thinking might include the addict or codependent being

- very rational about non-addictive issues, but highly irrational about addiction.
- extremely independent occupationally or functionally, but extremely dependent on a substance or a relationship.
- fearful of loneliness and abandonment, but also afraid to get close to anyone.

In this book, Dr. Twerski insightfully guides us through the origins and development of addictive thinking. He demonstrates how addictive thinking contributes to the addict's dilemma and how the therapist can successfully uncover the process of addictive thinking. Dr. Twerski has made enormous contributions to the understanding of the addictive process. This work is no exception. Addicts, codependents, and therapists will benefit as they begin to unravel the many mixed messages of addiction and codependency. This process begins by developing clear and logical thinking. It begins by identifying the dangers of *Addictive Thinking*.

ROBERT S. ACKERMAN, PH.D.

ADDICTIVE
THINKING

CHAPTER ONE

ADDICTOLOGIA, OR ADDICTIVE THINKING

"It Is Absolutely Impossible for Me
To Stop on My Own, Maybe"

I was interviewing a young man who had been admitted to a rehabilitation unit for drug addiction. "What made you decide it was time to do something about the problem?" I asked.

"I've been on cocaine for a few years," the man replied, "and on several occasions I didn't use for a few weeks at a time, but I had never before decided to stop for good.

"For the past year my wife has been pressuring me to stop completely. She used to do cocaine herself, but she has been off for several years now. I saw it wasn't worth the hassle, so I decided to give it up completely.

"I was sincere in my determination to stop for good, but after two weeks I started up again, and that proved something to me. I'm not stupid. I now know that it is absolutely impossible for me to stop on my own, maybe."

I wanted the man to hear what he had just said, so I repeated his last sentence several times. He could not see what I was trying to point out to him.

I said, "It is perfectly logical to say, 'Maybe I can stop by myself.' It is also perfectly logical to say, 'It is absolutely impossible for me to stop by myself.' But to say, 'I now know that it is *absolutely impossible* for me to stop on my own, *maybe*,' is an absurd statement because it is self-contradictory. It is either 'absolutely impossible,' or 'maybe,' but it cannot be both."

I have later repeated this conversation to a number of people, and even seasoned therapists initially show no reaction, waiting for me to give the punch line. Only after I point out the contradiction between "absolutely impossible" and "maybe" do they see the absurdity of the statement, and the distortion of thought taking place in this man's mind.

To understand what we are talking about when we use the term *distortion of thought,* let's look at an extreme example of it, the system of thinking used by a schizophrenic person. A system of thinking that is outside the realm of "normal" thinking is called *paralogia.* As absurd as this distortion of thought may be to a normal person, it makes perfect sense to a schizophrenic.

For example, in Aristotelian logic we use major and minor premises to lead to what we consider a valid conclusion. Thus:

Major Premise: All men are mortal.
Minor Premise: Socrates was a man.
Conclusion: Therefore, Socrates was mortal.

A schizophrenic might come up with this conclusion:

Major Premise: Socrates was a man.
Minor Premise: I am a man.
Conclusion: Therefore, I am Socrates.

The schizophrenic man in this example is as convinced that he is Socrates as the healthy person would be that Socrates was mortal. Therapists familiar with paranoid schizophrenic patients, who have delusions of grandcur, know how futile it is trying to convince a patient that he or she is not the Messiah or the victim of a worldwide conspiracy. The therapist and the patient are operating on two totally different wavelengths, with two completely different rules of thought. Normal thinking is as absurd to a schizophrenic as schizophrenic thinking is to a healthy person. A typical schizophrenic's adjustment to life in a normal society can be compared to that of a baseball manager who orders the team to punt or a football coach who calls for stealing a base.

Schizophrenic people do not realize their thinking processes are different from most other people. They can't see why others refuse to recognize them as a Messiah or the victim of a worldwide manhunt. Still, many people, some therapists included, may argue with a schizophrenic person, becoming frustrated when the person fails to see the validity of their arguments. They are unaware that this is like asking a color-blind person to distinguish colors.

Yet, the thinking of the schizophrenic is so obviously irrational that it is clearly recognized by most of us as irrational. We may be unable to communicate effectively with a schizophrenic person, but at least we are not taken in by the delusions created in the schizophrenic's mind. We do not believe this person is really the Messiah or the victim of a KGB, FBI, and CIA conspiracy.

How Addictive Diseases Resemble Schizophrenia

Not infrequently, persons with addictive diseases are misdiagnosed as schizophrenic. They may have

- delusions,
- hallucinations,

3

- inappropriate moods, and
- very abnormal behavior.

All of these may be manifestations of the toxic effects of chemicals on the brain. What these people have is a *chemically induced psychosis,* which may resemble but is not schizophrenia. Every so often, however, a person with bona fide schizophrenia uses alcohol or other drugs addictively. This presents a very difficult treatment problem. A schizophrenic is likely to require long-term maintenance on potent antipsychotic medications. This person might be unable to withstand the confrontational techniques that are commonly effective with addicts in treatment. Addicts can learn to desist from escapism and to use their skills to cope effectively with reality; no such demand can be made on a schizophrenic, who may lack the ability to cope with reality.

We may think of it in the following way. Both the addict and the schizophrenic are like derailed trains. With some effort, addicts can be put back onto the track. The schizophrenic can't be put back on the same track. The best that may be accomplished is getting a schizophrenic on another track that leads to the destination. This other track is not a "through" track. It has countless junctions and turnoffs, and at any point the schizophrenic may go off in a direction other than the desired one. Constant vigilance and guidance are necessary to avoid such turnoffs, and it may be necessary to slow the traveling speed with the use of medications to stay on track.

When we are confronted with the thinking of an alcoholic or someone with another addiction, we are often as frustrated as with the schizophrenic. Just as we are unable to budge the schizophrenic from the conviction of being a Messiah, so we are unable to budge an alcoholic from the belief that he or she is a safe, social drinker.

For instance, someone close enough to observe a late stage alcoholic (or other drug addict) can see a person whose life is steadily falling apart, with physical health deteriorating, family life in ruins, and job in jeopardy. All of these problems are obviously due to the effects of alcohol or other drugs, yet the person appears unable to recognize this. The addict may firmly believe that using chemicals has nothing to do with any of these problems and appears blind to logical arguments to the contrary.

An outstanding difference between addictive and schizophrenic thinking is this:

- *schizophrenic thinking* is blatantly absurd;
- *addictive thinking* has a superficial logic that can be very seductive and misleading.

Especially in the early stages of addiction, an addict's perspective and account of what is happening may appear reasonable on the surface. Many people are naturally taken in by addictive reasoning. Thus, an addict's family may see things the "addictive thinking way" for a long time. The addict may sound convincing to friends, pastor, employer, doctor, or even to a psychotherapist. Each statement the addict makes appears to hold up; long accounts of events may even appear valid.

The addict may not always be as willfully conniving as we think. This person is not necessarily consciously and purposely misleading others, though this does occur sometimes. Often addicts are taken in by their own thinking, actually deceiving themselves.

We all recognize the statement, "That full glass is empty," as absurd. But the young man's statement, "I now know that it is *absolutely impossible* for me to stop on my own, *maybe*," may not appear absurd until we stop to analyze it. In normal conversation, we generally do not have time to pause and analyze what we hear. Hence, we may be deceived by, and accept as reasonable, statements that are meaningless.

Sometimes these contradictions can be even more subtle. For example, a young woman, asked whether she had resolved all the conflicts connected with her divorce, answered, "I think so." There is nothing patently absurd about this woman's answer, until we pause to analyze it. The question was, "Have you *resolved* the conflicts?" This means, "Have you done away with the various uncertainties, and have you eliminated the emotional problems incidental to your divorce?" That is what the word *resolved* means. The answer, "I think so," is thus an assertion, "I am still uncertain that I am certain," and is really a meaningless statement.

In an article I wrote in 1974, I used the term alcologia to refer to alcoholic thinking. Perhaps the term addictologia is more appropriate now since it encompasses not only other chemical dependencies, but also other addictions with many similarities to alcoholism, such as eating disorders, compulsive gambling, and sexual addiction.

Cause and Effect

Does an addict's distorted thinking cause an addiction, or does the distorted thinking result from the addiction? Cause and effect in addiction cannot easily be determined. By the time an addict enters treatment, several cycles of cause and effect have usually occurred, and anyone trying to tell which is which may be caught up in a "Catch-22" (a no-win situation). Since we must begin somewhere, and since active addiction stands in the way of success in treatment, *abstinence must come first.* After prolonged abstinence, with the brain again functioning more normally, addicts can focus their attention on addictologia.

The phenomenon of abnormal thinking in addiction was first recognized in Alcoholics Anonymous, where the highly descriptive term *stinkin' thinking* was coined. Old-timers in AA use this term to describe the *dry drunk,* or the alcoholic who abstains from drinking but behaves in many other ways much like an active drinker.

The distortions of thinking are not unique to addictive disorders. These thought distortions can be found in people who may have other adjustment problems. But the intensity and regularity of addictologia is most common among addicts.

This book is intended to help the addicted or codependent person identify his or her thinking processes called addictologia. Additionally, it can help those working in the substance abuse field to develop a more comprehensive understanding of the impact thought processes have on

- the development and maintenance of addiction, and
- successful recovery.

CHAPTER TWO

DECEPTIVENESS OF ADDICTIVE THINKING

I cannot stress enough the importance of realizing that addicts are taken in by their own distorted thinking and that they are victims of this addictologia. If we fail to understand this, we may feel frustrated or angry.

Often when we hear the old using or drinking stories of recovering addicts, we laugh, because the absurdity of the addictive thinking and behavior can be hilarious. This, however, is a lot like the humor of watching someone slip on a banana peel. After the laughter is over, we realize that the person who fell could be seriously hurt. Similarly, while we do laugh at an addict's antics, we should also realize that this person suffered greatly during active addiction and that many people are still suffering.

"He Was Consuming Too Much Fluid"

One recovering alcoholic related how he was oblivious to the effects of his drinking, in spite of what people said to him. Since he drank only beer, this man was certain he did not have an alcohol problem.

Eventually this man began to be physically sick, and he could no longer deny that something was wrong. He concluded that by drinking half a case of beer daily, he was consuming too much *fluid*. So he switched to scotch and soda. When the physical symptoms got worse, he faulted the soda and switched to whiskey and water. As his symptoms got even worse, he eliminated *water*.

Is this rational thinking? Of course not. Can it be classified as psychotic thinking? Not by the current definition of *psychotic*, which is a general term for any major mental disorder characterized by derangement of personality and loss of contact with reality. But his thinking was clearly different from normal thinking.

Addictologia is not affected by intelligence. People functioning at the highest intellectual levels are as vulnerable to these thinking distortions as anyone else. In fact, people of unusually high intellect often have more intense degrees of addictologia. Thus, highly intellectual people may be the most difficult patients to treat.

The Attorney and the Turkey

A brilliant and highly skilled attorney adamantly refused to attend AA meetings, lest the exposure of his alcoholism jeopardize his career and standing in the community. But a visit from a grateful client who presented him with a dressed turkey for the forthcoming Thanksgiving Day changed his mind.

The attorney recalled leaving his office that afternoon, walking out into a cold rain, carrying the turkey wrapped in butcher paper. His next memory is coming to, while leaning against a downtown office building, holding a bare turkey under his arm, the paper bag washed away by the rain. Anyone seeing him would correctly assume he was drunk. Though he publicly appeared in this condition, he was too embarrassed to let someone see him walk into a church for an AA meeting.

Why didn't this man's brilliant analytical mind prevent him from such absurd reasoning? For the same reason that brilliant people are not immune to psychosis, neurosis, or depression. Once the psychological or physical craving for the chemical exists, it affects a person's thinking in much the same way as a bribe or other personal interest distorts one's judgment. The need for the chemical is so powerful that it directs the person's thought processes to sanction or preserve the drinking or using. The more brilliant a person is, the more ingenious are his or her reasons for drinking, for why he or she does not have to be totally abstinent, and for why the person considers AA or NA worthless organizations.

An understanding of addictologia can help us understand why some efforts at preventing alcoholism or other drug abuse fail. Most often, scare tactics are ineffective. Despite the well-publicized cocaine-related deaths of prominent people and extensive media education about the dangers of cocaine, many people are still enchanted by the drug's mystique. The noxious consequences, including the helplessness of the addiction, the enormous financial cost, the legal problems, the cocaine psychosis, and the high risk of death do not always register!

Addictologia, by blocking out certain facts, can exist even prior to the use of chemicals. Young people contemplating the use of cocaine, for instance, often suffer from it, taken in by promises of euphoria and not considering the terrible cost. Thus, addictologia cannot be completely blamed on the effects of chemicals on the brain.

Why Children Take Drugs, Why Parents Drink

Another characteristic of addictive thinking is that while it distorts the thinking of addicts about themselves, it may not

11

affect their attitudes toward others. Thus, an actively drinking alcoholic parent may be thoroughly frustrated as to why a son or daughter cannot understand the destructive effects of drugs. Likewise, a cocaine-using son or daughter cannot understand how a parent could return to drinking after a close brush with death due to the effects of alcohol.

Remember this, for it is important: *identification of addictive thinking must come from outside the addict.*

SELF-DECEPTION IN ADDICTOLOGIA

Everyone gets "taken in" by addictive thinking, but the person *most* affected by it is the one who is doing the deceptive thinking, the addict. The following stories illustrate this point.

"Entering Treatment Wouldn't Be Honest"

A fifty-five-year-old professional man consulted me following a confrontation about his alcoholism in which his ex-wife, four children, business partner, and two close friends participated. They confronted him with how his excessive drinking had affected their lives. The business partner, for example, threatened to dissolve the partnership because of the man's dishonest work habits.

The man claimed this intervention had "opened his eyes." Weeks earlier he had had a drunken-driving accident, but still he denied the problem. But when people cared enough for him to try to get him help, he realized he had to stop drinking. In fact, he hadn't had a drink in the ten days since the intervention.

I told the man his determination was a good beginning toward recovery, but determination alone could not stop his alcoholism. Treatment was absolutely necessary. I gave him the options of either (1) residential or (2) intensive nonresidential treatment.

The man, however, refused to enter a treatment program. Though he certainly didn't want to lose the affection and closeness of his family, or his business, he could not, in good faith, go to treatment. Why? Because he was certain he could now abstain from alcohol without outside help. So, if he entered treatment only to please his family and business partner when he knew he didn't need treatment, it would be dishonest of him, and *he was not about to do anything dishonest.*

My urge to burst out laughing because of the absurdity of this reasoning was tempered by my compassion for this man who was tragically deceiving himself. In many years of alcoholism, he had frequently lied to his family, friends, and business partner. He hadn't been honest for years. But to enter treatment was unthinkable because to do so would be "dishonest." This man actually believed that what prevented him from accepting help was his commitment to honesty! Such is the self-deception of addictologia.

"Only a Social Drinker"

Another example of addictologia is provided by a skilled cardiologist who drank heavily for years. As time and drinking went on, he began to experience *morning-after effects*. Although he got to the office and hospital daily, he felt sick until quite late in the morning. Still, he knew that he was "only a social drinker." He believed something was wrong with the way his stomach absorbed alcohol — too much alcohol was remaining in his stomach overnight.

The doctor remembered medical school, where students were paid to participate in experiments. One experiment he participated in involved a study of digestion. The student was given measured amounts of food, and forty-five minutes later a tube was passed through the nose into the stomach. Contents of the stomach were evacuated and submitted to the laboratory for analysis.

"I had become adept at passing a tube down my nose into my stomach," the doctor recalled, "and it occurred to me that this technique could be the answer to my early morning misery. Before going to bed at night, I would pass a tube into my stomach and empty its contents. As I expected, I woke up the next morning feeling much better. I continued this practice every night for six weeks. The only reason I stopped was the tube irritated my throat so that my larynx almost closed off, and I was afraid I would require a tracheotomy to breathe.

"But not even once," the doctor said, "not once in those six weeks did it ever occur to me that a social drinker doesn't have to pump his stomach every night!"

That is how treacherous the self-deception of addictologia can be. In the next chapter, we'll learn how such distorted thinking originates.

CHAPTER THREE

ORIGINS OF ADDICTIVE THINKING

How does addictologia develop? Why do some people develop healthy thinking processes and others develop thinking distortions?

I don't think we have all the answers. Furthermore, it is im portant to know that understanding how addictologia develops may be helpful in *preventing* addictologia and hence alcoholism and other drug addiction. But it is of limited value in treating and reversing the addictologia.

In general, theories of why a person became addicted don't help much in treatment. It is similar to fighting a fire. When the flames are raging, it is counterproductive to contemplate how the fire got started. At that point the only thing a person should do is put out the fire. Knowing how fires start is helpful in prevention, but not in managing the problem once it exists.

The most convincing theory on how addictive thinking develops was presented in a 1983 article by Dr. David Sedlak. Sedlak describes *addictive thinking as the inability of a person to make consistently healthy decisions in his or her own behalf.* He points out that this is not a moralistic failure of a person's willpower, but rather a *disease* of the will and *inability to use the will.* Sedlak stresses that this unique thinking disorder does not affect other kinds of reasoning. Thus, a person who develops a thinking disorder may be intelligent, intuitive, persuasive, and capable of valid philosophical and scientific reasoning. The peculiarity of addictive thinking, he says, is the *inability to reason with oneself.* This can apply to various emotional and behavioral problems, but is invariably found in addictions: alcoholism, other drug addiction, compulsive gambling, sexual addiction, eating disorders, and nicotine addiction.

How does this inability to reason with oneself develop? To understand, we must first recognize how the ability to reason develops. According to Sedlak, the ability to reason with oneself requires certain factors. First, a person must have adequate facts about reality. A person who does not know the damage alcohol or other drugs can do cannot reason correctly about their use.

Second, a person must have certain values and principles as grounds for making choices. People develop values and principles from their culture as well as from their home. For instance, if family or cultural values are based on physical attractiveness or expensive luxuries, these may determine a person's behavior; failure to obtain them can generate deep disappointment.

Third, and perhaps most important, the person must develop a healthy and undistorted self-concept. The psychiatrist, Silvano Arieti, suggests that small children feel extremely insecure and threatened in a huge and overwhelming world. A major source of children's security is reliance on adults, primarily parents. If children think their parents or other significant adults are irrational, unjust, and arbitrary, the anxiety is intolerable.

Therefore, children must maintain, at whatever cost, a conviction that the world is fair, just, and rational.

The truth, however, is that the world is often neither fair, nor just, nor rational. When anything happens that appears to be unfair, unjust, or irrational, children cannot afford to see it this way. They conclude instead that because the world "must be fair, just, and rational," *their perception* is faulty. They think, *I must not be able to judge things correctly. I am stupid.*

Similarly, even if children are treated, for whatever reason, in a manner they consider unjust, they are unable to believe the statement, *My parents are crazy. They punish me for no good reason.* This would be too terrifying a concept to tolerate. To preserve the notion that their parents are rational and predictable, their only option is to conclude, *I must somehow be bad to have been punished this way.*

As children grow up, these misconceptions may continue to color their thinking and behavior. They may continue to feel that they are bad people and undeserving of good things. Or they may consider their judgment grossly defective, which allows others to easily sway them.

A person can feel bad or worthless, even though this is a total contradiction to reality. Feeling insecure and inadequate makes a person more vulnerable to escapism, so often accomplished via mood-altering drugs. The person feels different from the rest of the world, as if he or she doesn't belong anywhere. Alcohol or other drugs, or other objects of addiction, anesthetize the pain and allow this person to feel a part of the "normal world." Indeed, many alcoholics or other addicts state they did not seek a "high," but only to feel normal.

Many thinking distortions are not necessarily related to chemical use. For example, fear of rejection, anxiety, isolation, and despair often result from low self-esteem. Many of the quirks of addictive thinking are psychological defenses against these painful feelings.

CHAPTER FOUR

THE ADDICTIVE THINKER'S CONCEPT OF TIME

I can quit any time I want.

If there were a contest for the most common sentence used by addicts, this one would win.

Anyone who has observed addicts knows they ''stop'' countless times and make innumerable resolutions. Abstinence may be for hours, days, or in some cases, weeks. But, ordinarily, before long the active practice of addiction resumes. This vicious cycle may continue for years.

Addicts simply are *unable* to stop any time they wish. Others can see this happening, but the addict does not. Family and friends may be bewildered, asking themselves, *How can a person insist that it's possible to stop at anytime when it's obviously not true?* Even seasoned therapists, used to this reasoning, may ask themselves, *How can an intelligent person be so utterly oblivious to reality? How can first-rate intellectuals with positions of great responsibility, who can analyze and retain scientific data, not add two plus two in regard to their addictive use of chemicals?*

The answer lies in an understanding of addictive thinking. Addicts are not as illogical as they appear if we understand one thing: the addictive thinker's concept of time. Addicts make perfectly good sense to themselves when they say, *I can quit any time I want.* We need to understand that an addict has a different concept of time from a non-addict.

Even for a perfectly rational person, time is variable. Under certain circumstances, a few minutes can seem an eternity, while under other circumstances, weeks and months appear to have lasted only moments.

"These Few Minutes Make Up an Addict's Future"

For the addict, time may be measured in minutes or even seconds. Certainly in the quest for the effect of a chemical, the addict thinks in terms of minutes. The concept I'm referring to is the addict's intolerance of delay for the sought-after effect. All of the substances the addict uses give their effect within seconds or minutes.

I have tried this approach with addicts in treatment who wish to leave treatment: I tell them that I have a "safe" pill that can give them a high equivalent to the "high" of cocaine and probably better. Then I give them a Vitamin B placebo. Twenty minutes later, they complain that they don't feel anything, at which time I say, "Oh, I forgot to tell you. The high doesn't come on for twenty-four to thirty-six hours, but once it comes on, it lasts much longer than the brief cocaine high, even up to a full day!"

Without fail, addicts refuse to wait for the "high," even if it might be better in quantity or quality. They leave treatment because they want an immediate effect. Incidentally, I then tell them that I gave them a placebo just to prove to them that a major part of their problem is impatience.

An addict who claims the ability to quit any *time* believes it is the truth. By abstaining for a day or two, the addict has stopped for a *time*. Indeed, having often abstained for several days, addicts may wonder why others cannot realize the obvious: they can "stop" any *time*.

You may tell the addict, "No, it's obvious that you cannot stop any time you want to." Your statement and the addict's statement, although seemingly contradictory, are both true. The key is that each person is using the word *time* differently.

We may become angry and frustrated with the addict. We wonder, *Why can't this person think normally? Why can't the addict think of future consequences?*

The addict does think about the future, but in terms of moments, not years. When drinking or using other drugs, the addict thinks the consequences are a glow, relaxation, detachment from the world, and perhaps sleep. This will all happen within a few minutes of drinking or using, and these few minutes make up an addict's future. Cirrhosis, brain damage, loss of job, loss of family, or other serious consequences are not likely to occur within minutes, so they do not exist in the addict's thoughts.

How different is the alcoholic from the smoker, who risks the consequences of serious circulatory problems, heart disease, emphysema, and cancer? The destructive effects of drinking or using other drugs may occur much sooner than those of smoking, but both the drinker and smoker are oblivious to the future. Similarly, people who are sexually promiscuous may be taking serious health risks, but again the consequences are in a "future" that is not in their conception of time.

A Culture with an Addict's Concept of Time

We are part of a culture that values the delivery of service in seconds — microwave ovens, television sets, and fast food restaurants all provide nearly instant gratification. We all, in some ways, operate with the addictive concept of time.

What about the cultural concept of the future? We've polluted the air, rivers, and oceans for short-term gain, disregarding long-range effects. We've destroyed forests and other habitats of endangered species with little regard for turning this world over to future generations. Are we not disregarding the future, very much as the addict does?

Understanding the Way an Addict Thinks

People involved with the Twelve Step program of Alcoholics Anonymous showed me how the misconception of time is prevalent in addictive thinking. Program people like to use the powerful slogans One Day at a Time and Time Takes Time to combat the forces of addictive thinking.

Recovering people intuitively know that one of the ways they must change their "stinkin' thinking" is to deal with their distorted concept of time. A convenient, manageable unit of time is *one day*. Often, however, people in early recovery must take it five minutes at a time and eventually work up to longer periods.

The idea of Time Takes Time is used to counter the addictive notion that time can happen fast, such as the addict who prays, "Please God, give me patience, but give it to me *right now!*" Again, the addict does not see any contradiction in this.

One of my patients wrote to me: "It is four years since I was taken into your office, utterly beaten, wanting to die, but not having the courage to take my own life. . . . The first two years, the only thing I did right was not drink and go to meetings. . . . I want you to know that it took me four years to finally feel different about myself."

When addicts recognize that part of their downfall was intolerance of delays and are willing to wait for the rewards of sobriety, they are on their way to recovery. If they want "instant" sobriety, they will get nowhere.

Old-timers in AA think of their sobriety in terms of twenty-four-hour segments. Sobriety anniversaries are celebrated, but with great caution. AAs know it's risky to think in terms of years rather than days. A popular AA guide, *Twelve Steps and Twelve Traditions*, refers to twelve-hour segments of time. Other literature recovering people like are meditation books that focus on a day-at-a-time approach, such as *Twenty-Four Hours a Day* and *One Day at a Time in Al-Anon*.

One Day at a Time is not just a clever slogan. It is absolutely necessary for recovery from addiction, as the next two stories illustrate.

"Nine Thousand, Eight Hundred And Thirty-Four Days"

I once asked an old-timer in recovery how long he had been sober. He reached into his pocket, took out a small diary, and after fingering the pages, looked up and said, "Nine thousand, eight hundred and thirty-four days."

Not understanding this, I asked, "What is that? Twenty-five or thirty years?"

With complete sincerity, he replied, "You know, doctor, I don't really know. You can afford to think in terms of years. I have to think in terms of days."

"Today You Have Been Sober Longer than I Have"

Acceptance of living One Day at a Time can also be seen in the story of a physician in her early recovery. The physician remarked to an AA old-timer that it must be a wonderful feeling to have been sober for so long.

The man looked at the woman and said, "You have been sober longer that I have."

"What on earth are you talking about?"

"What time did you get up today?" he asked.

"I had to be at surgery at seven, so I got up at five-thirty," she answered.

"There you have it," he replied. "I didn't get up until after seven. So today you have been sober longer than I have. I don't consider yesterday and the day before that. It's only One Day at a Time, and today you have been sober longer than I have."

Little wonder that when he died at age seventy-nine, he had achieved forty-three years of quality life and happy sobriety.

Conclusion

When addicts fully grasp the One Day at a Time concept, they have begun their recovery. They must proceed cautiously, however, because a recurrence of time distortion is reason to suspect the possibility of a relapse. The time dimension of thinking is thus an important consideration for both the recovering addict and the professional in understanding and managing addictive diseases.

CHAPTER FIVE

CAUSE AND EFFECT IN ADDICTIVE THINKING

"Alcoholic Thinking Is as Destructive as Alcoholic Drinking"

I once heard an AA speaker describe the way he used to think during his drinking days. The absurdity of his thinking was hilarious, and everyone enjoyed a good laugh. There was more laughter when the man suggested that alcoholic thinking is every bit as destructive as the alcoholic drinking. To illustrate, the man read the questions from a self-test for alcoholism, substituting the word *thinking* for the word *drinking*. Here is what he read:

ARE YOU AN ADDICTIVE THINKER?

1. Do you lose time from work due to *thinking?*
2. Is *thinking* making your home life unhappy?
3. Have you ever felt remorse after *thinking?*
4. Have you gotten into financial difficulties as a result of *thinking?*

25

5. Does your *thinking* make you careless of your family's welfare?
6. Has your ambition decreased since *thinking?*
7. Does *thinking* cause you to have difficulty with sleeping?
8. Has your efficiency decreased since *thinking?*
9. Is *thinking* jeopardizing your job or business?
10. Do you *think* to escape worries or troubles?

The point is that even in absence of chemicals, the distorted, addictive thinking causes havoc. One example of this is the reversal of ordinary cause and effect. Although addictive thinkers turn logic around, they are absolutely convinced that their logic is valid. They not only resist rational arguments to the contrary, but cannot understand why others do not see the "obvious."

An Addict's Version of Dyslexia

We might understand this better with a comparison to *dyslexia*. Some people who have this learning disorder "see" letters reversed in words. You show them the word *CAT* and ask them to spell it, and they may spell *TAC* or *CTA*. But they are certain they have spelled it accurately. The problem involves their perception of how the letters are organized. This does not reflect on their intelligence; dyslexia can occur in highly intelligent people.

Something similar happens when an addict mentally reverses cause and effect. For example, an addicted woman claims that she drinks and uses pills because her home life is intolerable. She is telling what she perceives to be the truth. Her husband has withdrawn from her, is unresponsive to her, and makes caustic comments. Her children are ashamed of her and treat her with disrespect. She believes this emotional torture causes her to drink. As one person said, "When work is over and you know you've already experienced your high for the day, and there's nothing to look forward to, of course you want a few drinks."

Whether it is the attitude of the family, pressure on the job, insensitivity of an authoritarian boss, callousness of friends, anxiety attacks, headache or nagging backache, a financial squeeze, or any other problem the addict claims is the reason for using chemicals, the formula is always the same. The fact is that *chemicals usually cause the problems*, but the addicted person believes that *problems cause chemical use*.

While the addicted woman in the example has the problems she complains about, she fails to recognize her confusion over cause and effect. Her husband's behavior, although unpleasant, is in response to her drinking and pill-taking. He cannot communicate meaningfully with her *because of her chemical use*. The children are angry and ashamed that they cannot invite friends over because they fear her unpredictable antics. They have lost respect for her *because of her chemical use*.

When you show a dyslexic the word *CAT* and he or she spells it *TAC*, it is because that is what the person honestly sees. Unless the dyslexia is corrected, it is unrealistic to expect this person to see otherwise. With an addicted person, perception of reality will continue to be distorted *with* or *without* active use of alcohol or other drugs until the distorted perception that accompanies addictive thinking is corrected.

CHAPTER SIX

HYPERSENSITIVITY OF ADDICTIVE THINKERS

To better understand the attitudes and reactions of the addict, it is important to know where this person is coming from. We can understand a person's extremely unusual reactions to a certain experience only if we understand the conditions surrounding the experience.

If we were to see someone reacting angrily to what appears to be hardly noticeable contact, say, brushing against someone in a crowded elevator, we would probably wonder, *What's wrong with that person?* Or we might think this person has a very short fuse. We would likely consider the angry reaction unwarranted.

Suppose, however, that the person involved had a blistering sunburn. The entire picture now changes. What appeared to be superficial contact was actually enough to elicit excruciating pain, and even if the angry outburst was not justified, at least we can understand why it occurred.

While a sunburn is apparent to everyone who can see, people's emotional sensitivities are not. We may therefore fail to understand an intense reaction if we are not aware of a person's peculiar sensitivities.

I have often wondered why some people resort to using alcohol and other drugs to feel better and others do not. Genetic and physiological differences in people play an important role in the development of addictions. But these are certainly not the entire answer.

Relief from Feelings of Distress and Discomfort

Though many people use alcohol and other drugs to get high, many others use just to feel normal. For these chemically dependent people, alcohol and other drugs are emotional anesthetics, relief from feelings of distress and discomfort.

Certainly just about everyone's life has plenty of stressful circumstances. Why, then, do so many people *not* use alcohol or other drugs to cope with their distress?

I believe some people have greater sensitivity to stress. These people apparently feel emotional discomfort more acutely than others.

I am convinced that addicts, more emotionally hypersensitive, are likely to have more intense emotions than non-addicts. Chemically dependent people often seem to be almost inordinately sensitive with emotions of extreme intensity. When they love, they love intensely, and when they hate, they hate intensely.

The emotional sensitivity of the addict may be similar to the hypersensitive skin of a sunburn victim. A stimulus that might not produce emotional pain in a non-addict can produce great distress in an addict.

Many addicts are loners. It would be easy to conclude that they are antisocial and enjoy solitude, but that isn't necessarily true. Human beings are by nature gregarious animals and crave companionship. The loner doesn't really enjoy isolation, but it is the lesser of two evils. Mingling with people exposes the addict to the possibility of rejection. While rejection wouldn't be pleasant for anyone, to the addict it is devastating. The addict often anticipates rejection, where someone else may not even think of it.

Earlier, I mentioned that distorted, addictive logic is not always a consequence of chemical use, but often precedes it. The same is true of emotional hypersensitivity.

"I Didn't Belong with Y'all"

A man in his nineteenth year of recovery said in an AA talk, "When I got to be about nine years old or so, I began to feel that I was different from y'all. I can't tell you *why* I felt different, but that is just the way I felt. If I walked into a room full of people, I felt I didn't belong with y'all, and that didn't feel good. I just didn't belong. Years later, when I took my first drink, I suddenly felt the world was right with me. I belonged."

This vividly illustrates the intensity of the feelings of being different that most addicts say they experienced even before they used their first drug.

As sensitive as a prickly sunburn may be, a sunburnt person knows that, although someone's touch may elicit sharp pain, usually no offense was intended. Hypersensitive addicts, however, often aren't aware of their extreme emotional sensitivity, so they see hostile intent in innocent acts or remarks and are apt to react accordingly.

When we observe some of the reactions of a person using addictive logic, let us keep in mind the example of the sunburnt person. It may help us better understand.

CHAPTER SEVEN

GUILT, SHAME, AND ADDICTIVE THINKING

It is commonly thought that addicts are guilt-ridden. Certainly when we hear an addicted person express remorse, we sense how deeply guilty this person feels.

Addicts may indeed feel genuine remorse, but often they feel not guilt but *shame*. There is a big difference.

The Difference Between Guilt and Shame

The main distinction between guilt and shame is this:

- The *guilty person* says, "I feel guilty for something I have done."
- The *shame-filled person* says, "I feel shame for what I *am*."

Why is the distinction so important? Because people can apologize, make restitution, make amends, and ask forgiveness for *what they have done;* they can do pathetically little about *what they are*. Alchemists during medieval times spent their working lives futilely trying to convert lead into gold. By

33

contrast, a person feeling shame thinks, *I cannot change my substance. If I am composed of inferior material, there is no reason for me to make any effort to change myself. It would be an act of futility.*

Guilt can lead to corrective action. Shame leads to resignation and despair.

Close analysis of addicted people often reveals very low self-esteem and deep-seated feelings of inferiority.

How Shame Develops

It is not always possible to discover in each addict how feelings of shame developed. Shame can develop as a result of many things: the book *Letting Go of Shame* by Ronald and Patricia Potter-Efron lists genetic and biochemical makeup, culture, family, shaming relationships, and self-shaming thoughts and behavior as sources of shame.* But one major contributing factor may be the way human beings come into the world. Humans are helpless and remain dependent longer than any other living being. Animal cubs run around when they are just days old, and weeks after birth many forage for their own food. Humans would die without adult care for the first several *years* of life. And even if they are physically self-sufficient, some offspring remain economically dependent on parents well into the third decade of life. Being dependent on others does not foster self-esteem. Helplessness and dependency can generate feelings of inferiority.

It takes enlightened effort by parents to help their children develop self-esteem. Parents who are overprotective or do too much for children do not allow them to develop a sense of mastery. Parents who make demands on children when they

---

*Ronald and Patricia Potter-Efron, *Letting Go of Shame: Understanding How Shame Affects Your Life* (Center City, Minn.: Hazelden Educational Materials, 1989), 2.

are not yet capable of fulfilling them can cause children to feel inadequate. Ideal parental and environmental circumstances are rare; thus, many people grow up with shaky self-esteem.

Why Addicts Feel Shame

The feeling of low self-esteem or shame in addicts is usually more severe. Circumstances that ordinarily cause feelings of guilt in emotionally healthy people bring feelings of shame to addicts as a kind of short-circuit. Suppose you turn the switch for the air conditioner and instead the lights go on, or you turn on the dishwasher and the garbage disposal starts up. Obviously the wires are crossed. That is what happens with addicts. What should produce guilt instead produces shame.

Shame in addicted people is not only unproductive but is also *counterproductive*. Suppose you had an automobile that was operating well, but a part became defective. You would replace the defective part, and the machine would operate well again. If, however, you found your car was a "lemon" and each time you corrected a problem something else went wrong, you might throw your hands up in disgust. You might justifiably conclude there is no purpose in getting the car repaired.

That is how the person with shame feels. Feeling shame instead of guilt is a characteristic of addictive thinking. The remorse of the addict is not a guilt trip; it reflects self-pity and shame. Destructive behavior makes this person feel defective, rotten to the core, and incapable of being anything else. With this attitude of despair and futility, it is easy to relapse into chemical use again.

Rokelle Lerner says that the Twelve Step programs convert *shame* into *guilt*. This statement contains much truth, but it is incomplete. The Twelve Step program not only converts shame into guilt. It also helps an addict deal constructively and effectively with the guilt.

CHAPTER EIGHT

MORBID EXPECTATIONS

Frequently, addictive thinkers, for no logical reason, will feel apprehensive, anticipating disaster.

Good and bad things happen in this world. Most people experience both. Addicts are not the only people who worry and anticipate negative happenings, but they tend to do this more often than other people.

Some people are optimists. When they see a heap of manure, they look for a pony. Other people are pessimists. When they see a beautiful buffet meal, they worry about food poisoning. Learning why people develop such opposing attitudes is not always easy.

Many addicted people are unable to see good in *good* happenings. Addictive thinkers seem burdened by a morbid feeling of being jinxed. When something good does happen, they feel it can't last. On one hand, addictive thinkers fear anything that appears to be working well will eventually fail. On the other hand, they go ahead and do the very thing that brings the failure they fear. Some addicted people have a pattern of building to the verge of success, and then sabotaging it.

It is important to understand this aspect of addictive thinking. Family and therapists may feel encouraged by the recovering person's success in business and apparent happiness. There may be no telltale signs that beneath this superficial happiness, the recovering person is thinking, *I can't make it*. Sometimes this nagging anticipation becomes so unbearable that the addict thinks, *Oh, what the hell, I might as well get it over with*, and then precipitates the failure.

If the recovering person were using normal logic, it would be reasonable to reassure him or her that everything is going well and that there is no reason to expect sudden reversal. But if the recovering person is still operating out of addictive logic (which does not disappear immediately with abstinence), reasonable arguments will have no effect. The addict in early recovery may seem outwardly agreeable when these issues are discussed logically, but another thought system is operating inside.

When we discuss methods of helping an addicted person, we will address this problem. For now, just be aware that addicts often feel they are walking under a dark cloud of impending doom.

CHAPTER NINE

OMNIPOTENCE AND IMPOTENCE

One feature of addictive thinking is the illusion of being in control. To some degree, a delusion of *omnipotence* (feeling one has unlimited power) is present in every addict.

Most people addicted to alcohol or other drugs eventually lose control over the chemical; yet they insist they can control it. Although their lives have become grossly unmanageable, they steadfastly insist they are still in charge. This inability to admit loss of control in defiance of reality is characteristic of addictologia. It must be overcome before a recovering person can admit and accept *powerlessness*, a required First Step in recovery.

Alcoholics may have many reasons why Alcoholics Anonymous is not for them. Frequently, I have heard the objection, "I've been to AA meetings. They talk about God all the time, and I'm an atheist. I don't believe in God, and that's why I cannot use AA."

My response to this is, "You are a bit confused, my friend. It's not that you don't believe there is a God. You *do* believe there is a God. The problem is, you think you're God."

The dominant culture in the United States is *monotheistic*, one that believes there can be only one God. Theoretically, then, most of us would say there could not be two omnipotent beings. As long as a person believes in his or her own omnipotence, it is impossible to accept a God or Higher Power.

Along with a delusion of omnipotence, addicts have an attitude and fantasy of *grandiosity*, another feature of addictive thinking. Grandiosity in addictologia exists in stark defiance of reality.

The "CEO" with No Keys

One client of mine, at one time a very successful business executive, suffered the all too familiar loss of family, business, and home. Sitting at the bar, he would cry into his beer, fantasizing that at any moment someone would walk in and offer him the position as chief executive officer of a major corporation.

This man eventually entered rehabilitation, and during his entire stay, he was full of grandiosity. Certain he was better than anyone else, he looked down his nose at everyone. He objected to the recommendation that after treatment he go to a halfway house, even though he had nowhere else to go. Grudgingly and condescendingly he went to the halfway house, still grandiose. Reality notwithstanding, he continued to believe he was the successful executive.

The moment of truth came after six weeks in the halfway house. He recalls it this way: "I was standing outdoors, with my hands in my pockets. Removing the contents of my right pocket, I found I had twelve cents and a trouser button. Then I felt in my left pocket, and it suddenly hit me that *I had no keys.* I didn't own anything I needed a key for. No apartment, no office, no car." Not until this point did he accept reality.

Grandiosity and the delusion of omnipotence often go together. Both may well be desperate efforts to avoid the awareness of *impotence*.

Human beings are, after all, impotent in many ways. Many things in life — the weather, other people, the price of milk — are beyond our control. Many parts of us, both physically and psychologically, are beyond our control.

People who feel good about themselves are not usually threatened by an awareness of their importance. But when people have no self-esteem, when they feel inadequate, incompetent, and worthless, they must protect themselves against what they see as another put-down: the inability to control chemicals. Building self-esteem can help recovering addicts overcome this subtle yet powerful threat.

CHAPTER TEN

ANGER

Anger is a powerful and important emotion. Its management may well be the most difficult psychological problem of our era. While addiction literature has some fine books on anger management, relatively little can help us understand the real essence of anger.

All emotions have a function. Although religionists and secularists disagree on many issues, they do agree that everything in nature has a function. For example, the vast array of colors in the animal world, from the multicolored birds to the splendor of aquatic life, all serve some purpose. Colors may allow a creature to blend into the environment, serving as camouflage for protection.

We might ask ourselves, *What is the functional value of anger in nature?* It does not seem necessary for survival. If I were attacked, I might be able to defend myself adequately without becoming angry. Fear can exist without anger and can initiate the flight or fight reaction necessary for survival. Even without anger, I could recall who attacked me and be alert to possible future attacks.

Anger is not the same as hatred. We can be very angry at someone we love, and we can hate something without being angry at it. Then what purpose does anger serve?

I believe a natural purpose of anger is to preserve social order. Our feelings of outrage at someone being robbed, beaten, or harmed prompts us to take action to prevent such happenings. Without anger, we might defend ourselves adequately, but we might not make the effort to protect anyone else. *Anger is an emotion that is evoked by the occurrence of injustice, toward ourselves or others.*

So what is unjust? That depends on what each person thinks. People differ sharply on what is just or unjust in this world. Thus, some people become angry much quicker than others.

Addicts and Intense Anger

Anger can be very destructive when it malfunctions. Though many people have problems with anger, addicts often have a particularly difficult time with their intense anger. Bringing anger under better control is necessary in recovery.

If anything seems to be present in nearly all addicts, it is the conviction that the world has been unfair. They feel victimized by everyone, and they are angry at everyone, including God. *Why me? Why are You doing this to me?* is a common refrain.

The sensitivity of the person with a blistering sunburn who may feel excruciating pain even when only touched lightly is much like the sensitivity of the addicted person to self-perceived injustice. Addicts often feel offended, belittled, and humiliated by everyone. Their families don't love them *enough*, their friends don't value their companionship *enough*, they don't get *enough* recognition from employers for their hard work, and so on. How much is *enough?* Given the hypersensitivity and the insatiable needs of some people, infinity may not be enough.

Distorted Perceptions

The problem, then, for addictive thinkers is not in the abnormality of their *reactions*, but in the distortion of their perceptions. An example is the man who becomes irate when he walks into a room where his children are watching an absorbing television program. They do not jump up to greet him. To the man, this is an indication of how little the children value him. A person who "breaks his neck" to provide adequately for the children should be appreciated more. To this man, lack of appreciation is a gross injustice, and he feels intense anger. When his wife shows attention to her friends, he feels she doesn't value him and becomes angry with her for humiliating him.

We can thus understand, although we don't excuse, the reactions of the addict who feels victimized by "injustice." Is it not accepted in every culture that perpetrators of injustices should be punished? That is what an addict who acts out anger is doing, punishing another for an "injustice." While techniques for managing anger are important, getting rid of the distorted thinking that generates the anger would obviously be most helpful.

How AA Can Help

Heightened sensitivity and resulting anger are often present in other personality disorders as well. The recovering addict may have an advantage over non-addicted people: a Twelve Step program such as AA offers help to deal with anger.

AA has long recognized the pivotal role of resentments in active alcoholism and the need for recovering people to rid themselves of resentments if they are to stay sober. Some AA slogans can be used to address this problem, as when Easy Does It is applied to avoiding emotional eruptions. Some AA ideas recognize the futility of anger. One is the saying, "Holding on to resentments is allowing someone else to live in your brain rent-free." These are valuable ideas, but still they do not get to the essence of the problem.

Reducing Hypersensitivity

Recovering people get rid of resentments when they develop a self-concept and self-esteem that reduces their hypersensitivity. Thus, when they begin to feel better about themselves, they no longer need constant reassurance that others love and respect them. The man in our example can understand that the children's absorption in a television program does not mean a lack of love and respect for him.

Repressing Anger

Sometimes anger is repressed. Sometimes it first emerges as other emotions, and those other emotions are converted to anger.

When sound waves strike our eardrums, we perceive sound. Similarly, when we feel an injustice has been done, we feel angry. The sensation of anger in response to injustice is perfectly normal.

But certain people have learned, in one way or another, not to feel anger. This repression of anger is not a control technique, where a person recognizes anger and decides to handle it in a certain way such as slowly counting to ten. *Repression* is a psychological mechanism that keeps a person from being aware of an unacceptable emotion or idea. At an unconscious level of the mind, anger may be felt, but it doesn't appear in the person's awareness.

"Feeling Anger Would Be Sinful"

A good example of this is a patient I treated for chronic depression. A nun with strict religious training, she had developed the idea that feeling anger is sinful.

To get to my office, Sister had to travel one and one-half hours via two buses. She wanted to avoid being late for her appointment, but the bus schedule was such that she arrived about an hour early. I tried to always be prompt, and she always waited patiently.

One time I had to unexpectedly leave town, and I neglected to tell my secretary to call Sister and cancel the appointment. I later learned that after waiting long beyond her appointment time, Sister asked about the delay and was told that I was not in the office that day.

On my return I called Sister, apologized, and set another appointment. When she came to my office, I again expressed my regret for failing to notify her of this cancellation in advance.

"I'm sure that when you found out I was not in, you were very angry," I said.

Sister smiled. "No. Why should I be angry?"

"Because you traveled for an hour and a half and then waited two more hours, and you wasted a great deal of time because I neglected to call you. There is no way you could not have been angry."

Sister continued to smile sweetly. "I understand that these things can happen. You are a very busy man. I have no reason to be angry."

"I'll do my own apologizing," I replied. "I appreciate your consideration and your willingness to overlook my mistake, but don't tell me you did not feel offended."

With the same sweet, smiling expression, Sister said, "No, why should I feel offended?"

I am certain Sister was telling the truth when she said she did not *feel* offended and did not *feel* angry. Feeling is a sensation, and her sensory system did not register anger. It had been trained that way.

I think there is something wrong with that. It's like discovering numerous burn marks on your hands and not recalling being burned. If your nervous system is intact, a burn should produce pain. If it does not, then there is something wrong.

Voluntarily controlling one's reaction to anger is not wrong. Certainly it is not necessary to throw things, to hit the wall, or to shout obscenities. In fact, those who say a person should discharge anger by screaming or even hitting a punching bag have little clinical grounds for this recommendation. It is perfectly safe to decide not to manifest anger. But not to *feel* anger is something else. Not feeling anger indicates an unconscious denial and *repression* of anger, and this can cause problems. Little wonder that Sister was chronically depressed and suffering from high blood pressure and ulcers. Anger that is denied and repressed can be converted into depression and various physical diseases.

The reverse can also occur: other emotions can be converted into anger. This often happens when people feel they must disown a particular emotion, such as when they think they must deny feeling pain.

Men Do and Should Cry

Ideas such as "men don't cry" are rather strange. But some men believe that it is masculine to be stoic, that feeling hurt is a sign of weakness. When something happens that should normally produce a sensation of emotional pain, such as being rejected by someone they love, they may respond with rage. But they cannot admit they feel hurt.

It is okay to be angry at injustice, and the cultural belief that a person dare not feel hurt is indeed unjust. Feeling hurt when rejected or slighted is normal, no matter your sex. To deny a person's right to feel and express pain is a gross injustice. We can thus understand, although not excuse, reactions of rage that may seem inappropriate. In these cases, learning new skills that allow a person to experience and express the proper emotion may eliminate inappropriate anger responses.

Recovering addicts learn how harmful harboring resentments can be. If they wish to avoid relapse, they must work on their anger and resentments. Non-addicted people may be less aware of this and, thus, more vulnerable to developing various physical and emotional problems. These may include migraine, high blood pressure, heart disease, peptic ulcers, and depression, which can result from repressing anger or harboring resentments.

People are not apt to consider being an addict highly desirable. But if we realize that the gains from recovery in a Twelve Step program may not be easily found in other ways, being addicted is certainly not the curse that we may have thought it to be.

CHAPTER ELEVEN

MANAGEMENT OF FEELINGS

Addicts may have great difficulty with their feelings. Negative feelings such as envy, greed, and hate are not the only ones difficult to manage. Even some positive feelings — for example, love, admiration, and pride — may baffle the addicted person, sometimes even more so *after* stopping chemical use.

Emotions are motivating forces; by definition, they are what make us move. They are akin to an automobile engine that provides the energy to propel the car.

Think of a situation in which the driver is actually afraid of operating the vehicle. Perhaps this driver is behind the wheel of a racing car that generates such power and high speeds that the driver can't maintain control. Or perhaps the driver believes the brakes are failing or the steering mechanism is malfunctioning. Whatever the case, the driver will be very reluctant to sit behind the wheel, fearing loss of control and an accident.

When people fear their emotions, two things are happening:

- their emotions are so intense as to feel uncontrollable, or
- they feel incapable of managing emotions of normal intensity. They doubt the reliability of their "brakes" and "steering mechanism."

While some chemically dependent people use alcohol or other drugs to get high, others use them to feel normal. Mood-altering drugs are essentially *emotional anesthetics*: they numb feelings. When people stop using chemicals, those emotions that were primarily numbed by the chemical are going to be keenly felt.

Depression

Depression is one of the painful feelings that the addict may have anesthetized with alcohol and other drugs. It is little wonder that a newly abstinent person is apt to feel depressed. Abstinence unmasks previous feelings of depression. And the clarity of mind that follows abstinence allows the person to see the havoc that alcohol and other drug use has wrought on family, job, financial status, and physical health.

A story illustrates this point.

The "Joy" of a Cigarette Burn

A young man of twenty-three was admitted to a treatment center after eight years of using alcohol, pain pills, sedatives, and amphetamines. On the day following his admission, he encountered me walking down the corridor and asked if he could have a few moments alone with me. He then fell on my shoulder and began crying bitterly. "I can't take it, Doc! I can't take it! It hurts so bad. I never felt pain like this before. Help me, Doc! Give me something. I can't take the way I feel."

After he calmed down, I told him about a woman who, in an automobile accident, severed nerves that carry sensations from the upper right arm to the brain. Surgeons tried to repair the nerves. During the weeks of convalescence, her right arm hung with no feeling, lifeless as a sack of cement. Depressed and discouraged, she thought she would never have use of her right arm again.

One day someone dropped a lit cigarette on her right hand, and she felt the pain of the burn. She jumped up and ecstatically screamed, "I can feel! I can feel! It hurts! I can feel!" To anyone else, the pain would probably have been unpleasant. To this young woman, pain was a joy because it indicated that her ability to feel was returning.

I told him that since age fifteen he had been living as a zombie, anesthetized with alcohol or other drugs and unable to feel any emotion. True, he had not felt much pain, but he couldn't have experienced many pleasant sensations either. Now that he was off drugs, he could feel the pain and joy of life again.*

Newly recovering addicts may thus experience much anxiety and panic when confronted with new feelings they have never learned to manage. They may believe being angry means feeling homicidal, loving means engulfing someone, being loved means being engulfed by someone, hating someone means alienating the whole world, and so on. Confronting these feelings is a formidable challenge.

Some people in early recovery fear having no control over a specific feeling. Not knowing how to isolate a particular feeling or manage it, they just shut off their whole feeling apparatus.

It is like finding a break in one of the water pipes in your home. If you cannot find the valve that controls the flow of water to that pipe, the only way to stop the leak may be to turn off the master valve that shuts off the water supply to the entire house.

---

*This story, in slightly different form, first appeared in *Self-Discovery in Recovery*, by Abraham J. Twerski and published by Hazelden Educational Materials, 1984.

Anger

Anger is the most commonly feared emotion. But by shutting off the master switch and turning off all feelings, the person may become zombie-like. Family members, anticipating the joys of recovery, may become perplexed and disappointed. Not understanding what is happening to the recovering person, family members may feel drinking or other drug use is the lesser of two evils.

It is important for therapists and family members to understand what may be happening within the newly recovering person. They must be aware that in addiction, *feelings* were the target of the chemicals; discontinuing the chemicals can result in emotional chaos, which may appear as emotional paralysis.

Learning to evaluate and manage feelings are major tasks. This will take time, with many trials and errors. The recovering person must have a great deal of patience, and those around this person may need even more.

CHAPTER TWELVE

DENIAL, RATIONALIZATION, AND PROJECTION

The three biggest elements in addictive thinking are denial, rationalization, and projection. Although people familiar with treatment of addictions are aware of the prevalence of these traits in addicts, there is nonetheless good reason for us to explore them in more detail. Progressive elimination of these distortions is a key to the recovering addict making improvements.

The term *denial* as we use it here could be misunderstood. Ordinarily, denying something that actually happened is thought of as lying. While addictive behavior does include lying, denial as it is used in addictologia does not mean telling lies. *Lying* is a willful and conscious distortion of facts or concealment of truth. A liar is aware of lying. The denial of an addictive thinker is neither conscious nor willful, and the addict sincerely believes that he or she is telling the truth.

I therefore consider denial and, for that matter, rationalization and projection, to be unconscious mechanisms. While they are often gross distortions of truth, they are the truth to the addict. The addict's behavior can be understood only in the light of the unconscious nature of these mechanisms. This is why confronting the denial, rationalization, and projection with facts to the contrary is ineffective. The following story will illustrate this point.

The Practical Joker's Trick Eyeglass Lenses

A practical joker arranges for an optician to grind a pair of trick eyeglass lenses. These powerful lenses can magnify an object fifty thousand times.

This practical joker walks into a university library and finds a very tired student who has taken off his glasses and is resting his head on his forearm, sleeping.

Here is the ideal victim. The joker quietly picks up the eyeglasses, replaces the normal lenses with the trick lenses, puts back the eyeglasses, and sits to watch the fun.

A few moments later, the student awakens and puts on his glasses. Just at that time, a mosquito flies toward him. The student lets out a bloodcurdling scream, drops his glasses, and tears out of the library in a panic.

Do you have any idea how ferocious a mosquito looks at fifty thousand times its actual size? How should a person react to seeing such a ''vicious monster'' heading straight for his or her head? Is this student overreacting? Is he crazy for running in panic from a mosquito?

Obviously, the student's behavior is perfectly normal. He has no reason to suspect that his perception of reality is distorted. His experience has been that whatever he sees is reality; he has no grounds to think otherwise.

To him, the monstrous creature attacking him was real and by far the most terrifying thing he had ever seen. Anyone who saw what the student saw would have reacted similarly. The inappropriateness of his response is due to an error in *perception,* an error he is unaware of.

What if the student had run into your room screaming about an indescribably monstrous creature from another planet being in the library? You might try to reassure him or offer to accompany him to the library. But neither plan is likely to work. He *knows* what is there. He tells you that if you are foolish enough to go to the library and risk being attacked by this "monster," you may go by yourself.

You do precisely that, and after a few moments return with the reassurance that there is no extraterrestrial creature in the library. You may convince the student to return to the library with you. He does so, sees no monster, and although thoroughly bewildered by the incident, sits down to study.

He puts on the eyeglasses, and this time a harmless fly, magnified fifty thousand times, is buzzing around. Again a scream, again a dash for his life, and again the talk of space monsters in the library.

The point should be clear: Unless you can discover the reason for the distortion, and unless you can show the student the trick lenses that caused his distorted perceptions, your arguments concerning the absurdity of his fears will be futile. You can even parade before him one hundred credible witnesses who will swear that no monsters inhabit the library. He knows what he saw, and he trusts his senses over the sworn testimony of even one hundred witnesses. He has no reason to question the truth of his perception.

Faulty Perceptions Protect the Addict From Awareness

This is how addicts think and behave. They react according to their perception. If their perceptions were valid, their behavior would be perfectly understandable. Unless we can show them that their perception is faulty, we cannot expect their reactions and behavior to change.

Given how important self-concept is in addictive diseases, I think that the addict's distorted perception of him- or herself is the biggest problem. All other distorted perceptions are secondary.

Denial, rationalization, and projection are *unconscious psychological defense mechanisms*. Their function is to protect the addict from some intolerable, unacceptable, and catastrophic awareness.

That psychological defense mechanisms can operate without our awareness should not surprise us. Certainly our physical defenses work without our awareness of their function. For example, when we sustain an injury, even a tiny cut, our system goes into a defensive posture to prevent the injury from threatening our life. White blood cells from remote parts of the body destroy bacteria that enters the wound, and the bone marrow promptly begins to produce tens of thousands more white blood cells to fight infection. The platelets and other blood coagulating substances begin to form a clot to prevent blood loss. The immune system is alerted and begins to produce antitoxins to fight disease-producing organisms. All this very complex activity occurs without our being aware of what is happening within. Even if we are aware of what is happening, we still can't stop the process.

Psychological defense mechanisms are no different. They do not go into action at our direction. We are unaware of their operation, and, until we gain an awareness of them through recovery, we can do nothing to stop them. It is therefore futile as well as nonsensical to tell an alcoholic or other chemically addicted person to "stop denying," "stop rationalizing," or "stop projecting."

During my internship, a patient I treated helped me understand the defensive nature of unconscious denial.

That Just Couldn't Happen to Me

The patient, a fifty-year-old woman, was admitted to the hospital for exploratory surgery because of a suspected tumor. She told the doctor that she was very active in community affairs and had assumed many important responsibilities. Although a tumor might mean cancer, it was important to her that she know the truth, since it would be unfair to many people and many organizations to continue carrying responsibilities if her health deteriorated. The doctor promised to be frank and reveal all the findings of surgery.

Surgery revealed she indeed had a cancerous tumor that had to be removed. Because the tumor showed some indications it had already spread, the patient would need to undergo chemotherapy. Complying with her request for complete truthfulness, the doctor had a frank talk with the patient, telling her that a malignant tumor had to be removed for the cancer to be arrested.

Thanking the doctor for being truthful, she stated that she would cooperate with whatever treatment was recommended. She spoke freely with the nurses and the staff about realizing that she had cancer.

Upon discharge from the hospital, she returned weekly for chemotherapy. She often remarked to hospital personnel how fortunate she was to be living in an era when science had provided a successful treatment for cancer. She appeared to be adjusting well, both physically and emotionally.

Some five or six months after her surgery, however, she began to have various symptoms. The cancer had spread in spite of the chemotherapy. Eventually she developed severe joint pain and shortness of breath and was admitted to the hospital for further treatment. I did the admission *workup* (an intensive diagnostic study) on her, during which she remarked to me, ''I can't understand what is wrong with you doctors. I've been coming here regularly, and you just haven't been able to find out what's wrong with me.''

The latter remark astonished me, since she had repeatedly referred to herself as having cancer. I realized that as long as she saw cancer as some kind of abstract concept, which did not pose an immediate threat to her life, she could accept the diagnosis. Once the condition began causing pain and shortness of breath, concrete evidence that she was deteriorating, she felt so threatened that her psychological system shut off realization of the truth. She was not intentionally lying or pretending; she actually did not believe that she had cancer.*

Denial as a Defense

If we look at denial as a defense, the question becomes obvious: defense against what? In the case cited, the woman couldn't accept the devastating realization that she had a fatal disease and that her life was soon to end.

In the case of an addicted person, what is so terrifying that the addict's psychological system opts to deny reality? The answer is that awareness of being an alcoholic or drug addict is beyond acceptance. Why?

- The person may feel stigmatized at being labeled an *alcoholic* or *addict.*
- The person may consider addiction to indicate a personality weakness or moral degeneracy.
- The person may think not being able to use alcohol or other drugs again is frightening.
- The person may not accept the concept of being powerless and not in control.

---

*This story, in slightly different form, first appeared in *It Happens to Doctors, Too,* by Abraham J. Twerski and published by Hazelden Educational Materials, 1984.

It could be a combination of these and other reasons, but the addicted person finds accepting the truth every bit as devastating as the woman did accepting the truth of her cancer. Until denial is overcome, addicts are not lying when they say they aren't dependent on chemicals. They are truly unaware of their dependency.

Rationalization and projection serve at least two main functions: (1) they reinforce denial, and (2) they preserve the status quo.

Rationalization

Rationalization is providing "good" reasons instead of the true reason. This defense is not exclusive to chemically dependent people, though addicts can be very adept at it. Note that rationalization means offering *good* reasons. This does not mean that all rationalizations are good reasons. Some are downright silly, but they can be made to sound reasonable. Rationalizations function to divert attention from true reasons. They not only divert others' attention from the truth, but also the addict's. As with denial, rationalization is an unconscious process — that is, the person is unaware of rationalizing.

A fairly reliable rule of thumb is that when people offer more than one reason for doing something, they are probably rationalizing. Usually the true reason for any action is a single one.

Because rationalizations sound reasonable, they are very deceptive. Any person can get taken in by them. An excellent example of rationalizing is given by Marie Lindquist in her book, *Holding Back: Why We Hide the Truth About Ourselves.*

I heard an example of this one night as I listened to a radio talk show. A woman called to complain about her nonexistent love life. "I go out," she said, "I'm active, I meet dozens of men, but none of them are interested in me because I'm short." The host, a highly intuitive man, cut her off in mid-protest. Short? *Short?* It seemed highly unlikely that shortness was the lady's real problem.

After a moment's pause, the host gently asked the woman how much she weighed. Defensiveness bristled through the phone wires. "That's not the problem," the woman snapped angrily. In this way, she unwittingly revealed what her problem was — extra pounds that left her feeling defensive and unlovable.

Even over the phone, the woman's problem was evident, just as it must have been to anyone meeting her. Yet she was only vaguely aware of the truth about herself. Like Garfield the cat, she had convinced herself that she wasn't overweight, just under-tall! She had pushed the real issue away so often, had spun such a complex web of denial and rationalization, that she had lost sight of the real issue. In her mind, the source of her problems was her shortness — which, of course, she was powerless to do anything about.*

In addiction, rationalization reinforces denial. The alcoholic might say:

I am not an alcoholic. I drink because. . .

With addictive reasoning, if a person has an apparently valid reason for drinking, this means that the person is not addicted.

Rationalizing also preserves the status quo, making the addict feel it is acceptable not to make necessary changes. This characteristic of addictologia can be operating long after denial has been overcome and an addict is abstinent. Allen's story is an example of how rationalization preserves the status quo.

---

*Marie Lindquist, *Holding Back: Why We Hide the Truth About Ourselves,* Center City, Minn.: Hazelden Educational Materials, 1987, 35-36.

Lost Love

Allen, a twenty-nine-year-old man, consulted me two years after he finished chemical dependency treatment. Although successfully staying abstinent, Allen was at an impasse. He had dropped out of college and was unsuccessful at holding a job. Allen typically did very well at work, but when his performance led to advancement or increased responsibility, he would leave the job.

Allen claimed to know exactly what his problem was. He had fallen in love with Linda, and they had become engaged. Linda's parents, however, objected to the marriage and convinced her to break off the relationship.

Although this had happened more than five years before, Allen still loved Linda and hadn't gotten over the rejection. He was still grieving the loss. The thing that held him back was his continuing attachment to Linda.

I believe that as painful as romantic rejections may be, people do get over them eventually. Why was Allen different?

For several sessions, Allen and I tried to analyze the relationship to Linda and his reaction to the rejection. I proposed a variety of theories, all of which sounded logical, but both Allen and I felt that they were not the correct interpretation of this problem.

One night, after a session with Allen, I had a dream that brought back memories. As a child, I especially liked boat rowing, but not being able to swim, I was not permitted to go out on a boat without an adult. So I would go to the pier where the boats were anchored, and while the boat was securely tethered to the pier, I would row to my heart's content. There was little danger in doing this because the boat could not go anywhere. While I rowed I would fantasize getting to the other side of the lake and discovering a hitherto unknown land. I would plant the American flag on this new frontier just as some explorers had done. It was quite a normal fantasy for a ten-year-old.

When I awoke, I remembered this dream, and Allen's situation became crystal clear to me. In my case, I was not being *held back* from my adventures by the tether to the pier. I needed that tether. I could risk drowning if the boat were to leave shore. That tether was vital to me because it was my security.

Allen's situation was similar. For whatever reasons, he was terribly insecure. On one hand, going to college or accepting advancement at work might result in failure, and he did not want to take that risk. On the other hand, he could not accept that his stagnation was due to his apprehension, because that would mean admitting that he was not assertive or brave enough.

What Allen did was similar to what I had done with the boat. Just as I had tied myself to the pier, Allen tied himself to an event in his life that he felt was holding him back. Because being rejected is painful and depressing, and because people often do lose motivation and initiative following a romantic rejection, this sounded perfectly reasonable to Allen and those around him. *Poor Allen. Isn't it a shame what happened to him? The poor boy cannot get over his unrequited love.*

Attributing his problem to the rejection by Linda was a rationalization. It was a good explanation why Allen could not get on with his life, but *it was not the true reason*. Efforts at understanding why Allen's relationship prevented him from resolving his grief were futile because they were addressing the wrong point. Like other rationalizations, "the rejection by Linda" rationalization was a smoke screen.

The truth is that Allen did not want to deal with his insecurities and anxieties. Only after I refused to even hear of Linda, and instead focused on his need to cope with the challenge of getting on with his life, did Allen make the changes he had been avoiding.

Projection

Projection is placing the blame on others for things we are really responsible for. Like rationalization, projection serves two functions:

1. It reinforces denial.

   - "I am not an alcoholic. She makes me drink," or
   - "If you had my boss, you'd use drugs too."

2. It helps preserve the status quo.

   - "Why should I make any changes? I am not the one at fault. Let others make the appropriate changes, and when they do so, I will not need to drink or use any other drug."

Blaming someone else seems to relieve an addict from the responsibility of making changes.

   - "As long as others do this to me, you cannot expect me to change."

Since the others are not likely to change, the drinking and other drug use can continue.

In this way, projection appears unique to addictologia. Suppose a person were beaten and suffered a fractured leg. Would the person not seek medical help just because he or she knew who did the beating? By knowing whose "fault" a problem is, addictive thinkers believe they can justify not doing anything to solve it.

These three biggest elements of addictologia — denial, rationalization, and projection — must be addressed at every stage of recovery. They may be present in layers, much like the layers of an onion. As one layer of denial, rationalization, and projection is peeled away, another is discovered underneath. The progressive elimination of these distortions of reality allows for improvement in recovery.

CHAPTER THIRTEEN

MANIPULATING OTHERS

A lot of addictive thinking may exist prior to the abuse of alcohol and other drugs. But there is one addictive thinking characteristic that appears to be generated by chemical addiction: manipulation.

Non-addicts are occasionally manipulative, and addicts may have manipulated other people before they began to drink or use other drugs. But with the use of alcohol and other drugs, the problem escalates. People are forced into lying, covering up, and manipulating. Addicted people develop expertise at manipulating, and over time, this becomes an ingrained character trait.

Manipulation may start as a defensive maneuver to explain away the use of alcohol and other drugs, or to cover up problems, or to create situations that will facilitate drinking or using. But sooner or later it takes on a life of its own. The addict manipulates just to manipulate and lies just to lie, even though there may be nothing to gain. Manipulation and lying, instead of being a means to an end, actually become ends in themselves!

I often caution people entering treatment that they must be careful not to con themselves. People might gain a temporary advantage by putting something over on others, but it's a hollow triumph when they con themselves. The victor is also the vanquished.

Early in recovery, some addicts claim to have a flash of insight. It suddenly strikes them how blind they have been to their addiction, and how selfish and inconsiderate they have been.

- "I am certainly not so stupid as to revert back to my destructive behavior now that I have become aware of it."

Having had this vision of truth, they may elect to leave treatment because they "no longer need it." Or if they do remain in treatment, they may become "therapists" for other patients, helping them to achieve a similar flash of insight.

Nonsense! Years of addictive thinking and behavior do not melt away overnight. In spite of addicts' protests of sincerity, they are manipulating. The tragedy is that addicts have conned themselves into believing they have achieved instant recovery.

An unwary therapist may be taken in by the addict's sudden insight. How wonderful not to have to laboriously chisel away at the mountain of denial as with other clients! What a relief to have someone who can promptly begin working on the important issues of recovery! Here is someone who is ready to do a Fourth Step (taking a moral inventory) in the second week of treatment, and a Fifth Step (sharing his or her life history with another person) on the very next day!

This is a person who takes a high-speed elevator rather than the Twelve Steps. Beware! This is pure manipulation. Odds are that this person will stop at the nearest bar on his or her way home from the treatment center.

It has been wisely said that a shortcut is often the quickest way to some place you weren't going. Why should a person take such a shortcut? Because in contrast to normal thinking, where people may use shortcuts to reach a goal faster, in addictive thinking the shortcut *is* the goal. It doesn't have to go anywhere in particular.

As with other aspects of addictologia, the addict's shortcuts and manipulations do not appear to be obviously absurd, and it is easy to get taken in. These manipulations do not disappear immediately with abstinence from chemicals. Much time must elapse and much work must be done before the recovering addict can overcome manipulative behavior.

CHAPTER FOURTEEN

DEALING WITH CONFLICT

It has been said that the difference between *psychosis* and *neurosis* is that the psychotic says, "Two plus two equals five," while the neurotic says, "Two plus two equals four, and I can't stand it."

The non-addict accepts that two plus two equals four and adjusts to this without too much difficulty. The addict, too, may adjust well at times. But at other times the chemical makes the addict psychotic, and at still other times makes the addict neurotic. When reality seems too unbearable, the addict neither adjusts to it nor fantasizes it away. Rather, an actively practicing addict uses chemicals and becomes oblivious to reality.

With abstinence, an addicted person must face reality without the escape chemicals offer. This may help us understand why families of addicts, who may have long been demanding that the addict stop using drugs, are sometimes disappointed when this finally happens. The abstinent addict who has not had help in overcoming addictologia may be harder to live with than a practicing addict. It is not unheard of for families to nudge an addict into drinking or using again.

Ordinarily addicts do not have more conflict in their lives than anyone else — that is, *before* chemical use messes everything up. Once the addiction is well under way, the chemically confused mind can generate a lot of conflict. Overwhelming conflict is not responsible for chemical dependency. Rather, it is the addict's distorted perception that makes reality unacceptable.

The biggest distortion is in the addicts' self-image. In one or more ways, the addict feels grossly inadequate.

- A drug-addicted young woman, who is very attractive, will not date or look at herself in the mirror because she believes she is ugly.
- A man who is chemically dependent and the author of a textbook on medical pathology is extremely anxious lecturing to physicians because he's afraid someone might disagree with him, although he is the acknowledged international authority.
- An alcoholic, a highly skilled attorney, lives in terror because she thinks what she is doing isn't good enough. "My life is like walking through a mine field," she says.

When the layers of veneer are peeled off, an addict has extremely low self-esteem. If the distorted self-concept of an addictive thinker is not corrected, it will be difficult or impossible to maintain recovery. The addict could develop psychosis, neurosis, or a substitute addiction.

The misconception addicts have of themselves precedes the development of a chemical dependency, often by many years. The low self-esteem that comes with the use of chemicals is of a different kind — it is not related to a misconception about reality. There is nothing elevating about forgetting what happened yesterday, having a hangover, being a public spectacle, or waking up in jail. These are legitimate reasons addicts might develop low self-esteem.

Changing the negative self-image of an addict, the low self-esteem that *preceded* chemical use, requires that the addict believes he or she really is an adequate person. This is a major challenge for persons whose lives are in ruins. And we must remember that it is not only the low self-esteem of this "ruined" person that needs correction, but even that of the *pre-*"ruined" person. Addicts find escape in chemicals because they feel they cannot cope. They must learn they do have healthy coping capabilities. The following story shows how, deep down, the ability to cope with conflict is already there.

Becoming Aware of What's Already There

Once as I sat down to pay my monthly bills, I was terribly upset to discover that there wasn't enough money in the checking account. I racked my brain to figure where the money had gone, but to no avail. I was left with the options of (1) taking out a loan, or (2) letting bills go unpaid that month. Neither option was pleasant, but I chose the second.

About ten days later my bank statement arrived, and I was pleasantly surprised to discover there was more money in the bank account than I had thought. I had simply forgotten to record a deposit. There was no need for me to have been upset or to take out a loan.

My problem was that, though I did have adequate funds to pay my bills, I was unaware of this. My perception of reality was incorrect. I had to become aware that I did not need a loan.

In the same way, addictive thinkers need to become aware of what is already there. They invariably have the ability to cope with conflicts, once they become aware that they have this ability.

In my example with the checking account, this was accomplished very simply. The statement from the bank revealed my error and my misconception of reality. In the case of the addict, it is much, much more complicated. We may be faced with a person who is now say, forty-two, who has had self-doubts since the age of three. Much time and effort will be needed to undo that misconception. Remember, to the addict, *this misconception is reality.*

The Either/Or Rule

Addictologia is often also characterized by a rigidity of thought, what we may call *the either/or rule.* The addicted person is likely to think in extremes, with little understanding that there is flexibility in resolution of problems.

For example, a newly recovering husband may not be able to decide whether to divorce or to stay with his wife. He could try a temporary separation while he begins to work on his sobriety and his wife gets counseling, but this alternative has probably never occurred to him.

This lack of flexibility or consideration of alternatives causes a lot of frustration, because the person may not be comfortable with either "extreme choice." Why other options and intermediate possibilities between extremes do not occur to an addictive thinker is not clear.

Still, the addict's logic does not appear faulty. If there were only the two choices, both unsatisfactory, frustration would be justified. If you were unaware of the nature of addictive thinking, you could get taken in and share the addict's frustration when conflicts arise.

CHAPTER FIFTEEN

FLAVORS AND COLORS
OF REALITY

Frequently, even when seeing reality accurately, an addict will feel that reality is just not good enough. The normal rewards and pleasures of life are just not enough. Something is missing, and the addict feels cheated out of the true pleasures. Other people who appear to be content must be experiencing the "real" thing, but somehow, the addictive thinker feels deprived of this. *There must be more to life*, the addict thinks.

"I Cannot Stand Everything Being Gray"

Clancy, a popular AA speaker, says it so well: "My world was drab and gray. My wife, my job, my children, my car all were gray. I cannot stand everything being gray. I need color! And alcohol provided color to life." To the alcoholic or other addict, life is like food cooked without seasoning: tasteless and unpalatable.

A sensory experience is personal and subjective. It is almost impossible to communicate your sensory experience to another person or to quantify it objectively. If two people taste the same dish, hear the same melody, or see the same sunset, there is no way that one can know *exactly* what the other is feeling.

Similarly, when non-addicts try to understand the addict's use of chemicals, they may be at a loss. *What in heaven's name is wrong with this person who has a fine home, a good marriage, healthy children, and a rewarding job?* they ask themselves. *Why the dissatisfaction? Why does this person drink so much?* The answers may not be easy to accept.

- *Why does this person drink so much?* Alcoholics drink because they have the disease of alcoholism. They have lost control over their drinking due to this disease.
- *Why the dissatisfaction?* An addictive thinker's outlook on reality is distorted. Being chronically dissatisfied, addictive thinkers do not feel they are experiencing what they should experience. Life is not providing enough gratification, and alcohol or other chemicals seem to bring color to it all. The grays seem to change into dazzling colors. Now they feel what others must be experiencing in life. They feel *normal.*

When the chemical is taken from the addict, the addict faces symptoms of withdrawal. After these pass, the doldrums set in. The world seems gray again, devoid of color, of interest, of excitement, and of pleasure. Addicts entering recovery must realize that abstaining from chemicals will not be enough to make everything rosy.

If the addict should consult a psychiatrist, the addict's symptoms may appear similar to those of a depressed person suffering from a *major affective* (emotional) *disorder:*

- loss of interest in life,
- inability to concentrate,
- a feeling of futility,

- a low sex drive, and
- a feeling that life isn't worth living.

Little wonder that psychiatrists often diagnose the condition as a major affective disorder and prescribe antidepressant medication. In newly recovering addicts, these medications are notoriously ineffective and can be threatening to sobriety.

While the symptoms of the recovering addict and the person with a major affective disorder can be similar, there is an important difference.

With a major affective disorder sufferer, the symptoms have a fairly well-defined beginning. The person previously enjoyed life, was active, had interests until some particular time when things began to change. Sometimes the change can be related to either a physical event such as childbirth, menopause, surgery, or a severe virus, or to an emotional incident such as a financial reversal, death of a loved one, or, strangely enough, a promotion at work. The important point is that the change in the person's feelings and attitudes can be traced to a time, perhaps several weeks or several months ago.

With an addict, the "depressive" symptoms often do not appear to have even an approximate beginning. Many times the person always felt that way, even as an adolescent. Addicts are likely to say they never believed they had a fair shake and that everyone else always had more or better things. They may have been thought of as thrill-seekers or hell-raisers. More often than not, addicts will say they had been dissatisfied with life for as long as they can remember.

This kind of depression is not relieved by antidepressant medications. All they are likely to do is produce annoying side effects. Although tricyclic antidepressants and MAOI antidepressants are of no value in characterological depressions as those I described, these antidepressants are not addictive. The danger of addiction is when drugs such as Xanax, Tranxene, Ativan, and

Valium are used for depression. The tranquilizing drugs that are often prescribed may indeed temporarily relieve an addict's symptoms of depression just as the alcohol or other chemicals did, but they carry a very high risk of addiction in themselves. Unwittingly, the doctor may have substituted one addiction for another.

An addictive thinker may suffer chronic dissatisfaction. This could be due to unrealistic expectations rather than actual deprivation. This person may need the help of a therapist in clarifying reality. A most effective therapy can be a group experience, where, under guidance of a skilled therapist, an addict can begin identifying with others in the group and observing *their* distortions. The addict may become aware that he or she, too, might have been distorting reality. Seeing other people who also had unrealistic expectations can help the addict become aware of his or her own equally unrealistic expectations. Perhaps the world isn't all drab and gray, but it isn't all dazzling colors either.

The addicted person has often shut off an entire feeling system to avoid certain unpleasant feelings. As the addict is helped to realize this, he or she begins to understand that much of the darkness and gray was due to a sensory blockage. As the person becomes more comfortable with feelings and dismantles this massive defense system, he or she begins to appreciate some of the color and excitement that does exist in the world.

CHAPTER SIXTEEN

REACHING BOTTOM

True recovery from addiction means more than simple abstinence. It means relinquishing the pathological thought system
and adopting a healthy one. Since addiction involves a distortion of perception, only some major event or series of events
can make the addict question the validity of his or her perception. The event or events that bring about this breakthrough
are sometimes referred to as a *rock-bottom experience*.

Rock bottom can be variable. One woman hit rock bottom
when her husband decided to leave the relationship. One man
continued to drink after his wife and children left him, after
he lost a lucrative job, his home and car, and even after he sold
his blood to buy alcohol. Why rock bottom is different for different people can best be understood if we are aware of certain
behavioral laws.

The Law of Human Gravity

A law of human behavior that appears as inviolable as the
law of gravity might well be called the *law of human gravity*.
The law states, *A person gravitates from a condition that*

appears to be one of greater distress to a condition that appears to be one of lesser distress, and never in the reverse direction. According to this law, it is *impossible* for a person to choose greater distress.

What about martyrs who allow themselves to be tortured or killed for a cause? Are they not choosing a greater distress? For some people, transgressing a belief or principle that is very dear is a fate worse than pain or death. Martyrs choose what is *for them* a lesser distress.

greater distress

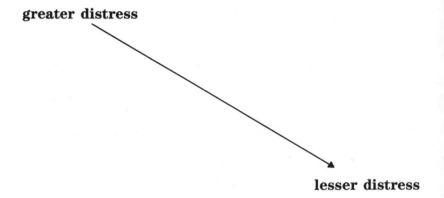

lesser distress

Any attempt to reverse the direction of the choice will be as futile as trying to make water flow uphill.

Alcohol and other mind-altering chemicals provide some measure of relief from discomfort, whether this is relief from anxiety, depression, loneliness, self-consciousness, or just the compulsive urge. Abstinence, at least initially, causes distress, sometimes psychological discomfort, and often severe physical discomfort.

If we try to get addicted people to stop alcohol or other chemical use, we are essentially asking them to choose a greater distress. But it is beyond human capacity to choose a greater distress. From this analysis it would appear that we should stop all efforts at treatment! Treatment can't work! But we know for a fact that treatment does work and that people do achieve sobriety. How does this happen?

Achieving Sobriety Through Changes in Perception

While the law of human gravity is inviolable, and the direction can never change, it is possible for people to change their *perceptions*. People can learn to see use of chemicals as the greater distress and abstinence as the lesser distress.

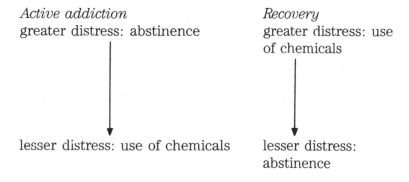

Active addiction
greater distress: abstinence

lesser distress: use of chemicals

Recovery
greater distress: use of chemicals

lesser distress: abstinence

How does this change of perception come about?

All mind-altering chemicals sooner or later cause some kind of discomfort. This may be

- hangovers,
- hallucinations,
- severe gastrointestinal symptoms,
- falls and bruises,
- convulsive seizures,
- the distress of poor memory,
- the loss of respect from family and friends,
- the threat of losing a job,
- the threat of imprisonment, and
- the terror of delusions.

81

When any of these, alone or in combination, reach the critical point where the misery equals or exceeds whatever relief the chemical provides, then the person's perception of what is a greater or lesser distress changes.

This, then, is what happens when rock bottom occurs. *Rock bottom is nothing more than a change of perception, where abstinence is seen as a lesser distress than use of chemicals.* If at any time after abstinence is achieved, even many years later, abstinence becomes the greater distress, relapse will occur.

The natural course of addiction is such that rock bottom will come if no one interferes. But people in the addict's environment, with every good intention, do things that they feel are helpful, removing some of the distresses that the chemical would produce. This prevents a change in perception of greater and lesser distress and permits the active addiction to continue. This is why people who remove the distressful consequences of chemical use are referred to as *enablers*.

Remember, allowing the natural unpleasant consequences to occur is not the same as punishing the user. *Punishing* is inflicting pain from the outside. If, for example, one partner in a marriage punishes the other for alcoholic drinking, then the marriage will seem to cause the greater distress. Only when the alcoholic discovers that alcohol is causing the misery, will being sober become a solution to ending the misery.

Addicts' perceptions also change when they see the rewards of abstinence. When the rewards of abstinence begin to exceed the rewards of mind-altering chemicals, addicts can change their perceptions of which is the greater or lesser distress.

Coming in contact with people who have sobriety and seeing that they are happy and productive demonstrates the rewards of abstinence. Getting the proper response to sobriety from family, friends, and an employer is a reward. Regaining self-esteem is a reward. Retaining one's job is a reward.

The active addict may recognize all these as rewards yet feel they are beyond reach. This is where competent therapy, with realistic and appropriate self-esteem building, can make a difference. With proper help, the addict may begin to believe that these rewards are achievable and perceive abstinence as the lesser distress.

People vary greatly in their perceptions of rewards and of misery. A therapist can learn what each person defines as *rewards* and *misery* in order to help the person put addiction and abstinence in proper perspective. The combination of rock bottom experiences plus realistic anticipation of the benefits of abstinence can make sobriety possible.

CHAPTER SEVENTEEN

ADDICTIVE THINKERS AND TRUST

Many techniques exist that treatment professionals and others can use to gain the trust of an addict, but whatever the method, successful treatment depends on the addict's trust.

Let's realize what we are asking of the addicted person. First, we are asking this person to completely and permanently abstain from use of the chemical that has made life livable, maybe the *only* thing that has made it tolerable. This is a very big thing to ask of someone.

"I Would Have Chosen to Drink and Die"

A bright recovering attorney said to me on his tenth anniversary of sobriety, "Doctor, when I was in detox and you showed me my physical exam and the lab tests, and you explained that if I didn't stop drinking I would soon die, that didn't faze me. I would have chosen to drink and to die. I could not conceive of living without alcohol when I needed it."

Abstinence is often a formidable challenge. But even abstinence is not recovery, only a prerequisite to recovery. Recovery requires a change in attitude and behavior, which means a change in the way the addicted person thinks and has thought for most of his or her life. It means overcoming addictologia. The formula can be shown as follows:

Recovery = Abstinence + Change.

Why It's Difficult to Convince Addicts Of the Fallacy of Their Thinking

Think, for a moment, what would happen if someone you trusted told you to take something precious, such as a fine crystal vase or a valuable porcelain sculpture, and drop it from a fourth-floor window onto a sidewalk below. You might say, ''Are you crazy? That's a family heirloom. It's priceless to me. Why should I do such a foolish thing and break it?''

Imagine your friend replying, ''Aha! That's where you're wrong. You see, you've been operating under this delusion that there is a law of gravity and that when you let go of things they fall downward. But you've been the victim of deception. There is no such thing as a law of gravity. Trust me, my friend. You'll see that if you extend that vase or sculpture out the window and let go of it, it will not drop to the ground. It will remain suspended in the air, and you can retrieve it anytime you wish.''

No doubt you will conclude that your trusted friend has flipped. *The poor person is insane!* you tell yourself. *I have always known that when I let go of things they do fall, and there is a law of gravity. This poor lunatic friend of mine is trying to convince me of the greatest absurdity. How crazy can a person get?*

When we try to convince addicts of the fallacy of their thinking, it is like telling someone that his or her belief in the law of gravity is a delusion. It is the height of futility to expect the person who has been an addictive thinker for most of life to abandon that concept of reality and accept ours instead.

Two Essential Factors in Recovery

How, then, can recovery ever occur? There are two essential factors.

1. Addicts Must Lose Faith in Their Current Reasoning Power
They must learn their concept of reality and thought processes are distorted. Unfortunately, others can do little to cause the addicted person to doubt a lifelong thinking pattern. *The only thing that will cause the addict to doubt is a rock-bottom experience.*

At such time, a therapist or professional can move in and say, "Look, you are becoming aware that your perception of reality is incorrect and that your ways of thinking are distorted. I will provide you with a valid system of thinking."

2. Addicts Can Accept the Possibility of Another Version Of Reality from Someone They Trust
I try to help patients in treatment understand this "reality check" by giving them the example of a person who is an excellent cook but has always cooked by tasting, never by following the recipe. The person doesn't know about quantities of ingredients. After putting in the ingredients, the cook tastes the concoction and adds salt, sugar, lemon, and spices, continuing to taste the mixture periodically, always adding what is missing until it tastes right.

But what happens if this person develops a severe head cold with clogged sinuses and is unable to taste anything? Since the cook doesn't rely on measurements, the next best thing is to call someone and ask, "Could you please come over and taste this for me and tell me what you think it needs? I have a bad cold and cannot taste anything."

For addicts, a treatment staff can provide this function. The addict's "taste buds" for assessing reality are not functioning properly. A treatment professional can help the addict to assess reality and develop a correct system of thinking.

But isn't this a bit much, to trust a person the addict has never seen before?

Most addicts lack an ability to trust. If they grew up in the home of an alcoholic parent, they had little opportunity to learn trust. Home could have been filled with lies and deception. The drinking parent lied to the sober parent; the sober parent deceived the drinking parent. Most children of alcoholics learned no one can be trusted.

Even children who grew up in healthy, functioning homes may have problems trusting others. Parents are not always forthright with their children for many reasons. Parents often think a child can't understand some things. So instead of telling the truth, they concoct something they think the child can grasp.

When an addict encounters a treatment professional, there may be little reason to trust. The rock-bottom experience may have pulled the foundation from beneath the addict, leaving the person suspended as if in midair. A treatment staff person shakes hands with the addict and says, "We will try to help you." *Big deal!*

If addicts have so little trust, how do they accept treatment from doctors or dentists? Or submit themselves to surgery? The answer is that these professional helpers are not saying things that contradict what the addict already believes. The surgeon says the addict's appendix is inflamed and must be removed; the addict never believed that an inflamed appendix should *not* be removed.

Treatment for chemical addiction is different. The addict will have to begin thinking in new ways in recovery, and that calls for profound trust.

Addicts in treatment must have reason to believe they won't be misled, that their welfare is the prime goal of treatment, and that nothing can deter the staff from that goal. Treatment staff may seek alliances with the addict's family, employer, or the court system, but only with a client's knowledge.

People in treatment for chemical dependency test those treating them, as well they should. Treatment staff tell them that much, if not everything, they believed until now is wrong, that their thinking has been distorted and is incorrect, and that they should rely on someone else's thinking.

Many residential treatment programs are of four weeks' duration. But we can't expect many years of addictologic thinking to reverse in twenty-eight days. All that can be provided in twenty-eight days is a place for the addict to start.

What Happens If Addictive Thinking Isn't Addressed in Treatment?

Let's say a newly sober addict leaves a treatment program after a period of enforced abstinence in which he or she has overcome physical withdrawal. If this person immediately resumes use of alcohol or other drugs, it indicates that the person did not begin to change his or her addictive thinking. No person thinking clearly would want to promptly return to active addiction. The conclusion is the person *remained addictologic.*

This, in turn, almost always means that the therapist failed to gain the trust of the client. This would not necessarily be a reflection on the treatment therapist's skills and dedication. The person may have entered treatment with a deep sense of distrust and is unable to trust anyone — yet. In spite of all that has happened, the person may not yet have reached the particular rock-bottom experience that could begin to break down addictive thinking.

What has been said about trust applies to everyone who wishes to relate to the addict constructively. This includes not only the therapist, but also family members, employer, pastor, sponsor, and friends in the recovery program. Each can earn trust, respect it, and guard it carefully.

CHAPTER EIGHTEEN

SPIRITUALITY AND SPIRITUAL EMPTINESS*

Although almost every human disease can be found among animals, there is no evidence that animals in their normal habitat develop addictive diseases. Some animals whose brains have been treated with certain chemicals may eat or drink excessively. But this does not occur in animals in their normal environments. Indulgence in excesses appears to be a uniquely human phenomenon. Why?

In contrast to animals, which have only physical urges and desires, human beings crave spiritual fulfillment as well. When this spiritual need goes unmet, a human feels vague unrest. While the necessary objects to satisfy hunger, thirst, or sex drive are easily identified, spiritual craving is harder to recognize and fulfill. The person has a feeling that something is missing, but does not know what that something is.

---

*The ideas discussed in this chapter are from *Animals and Angels: Spirituality and Recovery*, by Abraham J. Twerski and published by Hazelden Educational Materials, 1990.

It should not come as a surprise that spirituality, too, is subject to addictive distortion.

Why Other Objects Won't Quench This Vague Craving

Since previous experiences show that certain substances do produce a sense of gratification, addictive thinking leads the person to try to use food or alcohol or other drugs or sex or money to quench this vague craving. These objects may give some gratification, but they do nothing to solve the basic problem: the person's unmet spiritual needs. The feeling of satisfaction disappears soon, replaced by the ill-at-ease feeling.

Think of it this way. Humans require certain amounts of vitamins A, B complex, C, D, E, and K to function normally. A lack of any of these vitamins will result in specific deficiency syndromes, such as scurvy with vitamin C deficiency or beriberi with vitamin B-1 deficiency. If a person lacks vitamin B-1 and is given massive doses of vitamin C, the deficiency disease will remain unchanged. Nothing can change until the specific vitamin needed is supplied. You cannot compensate for a deficiency of one vitamin with excess of another.

This is similar to the mistake addicts make. The addictive thinker reasons that since alcohol or other drugs or food or sex or money have satisfied *some* cravings, they will satisfy *other* needs.

This also helps us understand the phenomenon of *switching addictions*, for instance, switching an eating disorder for compulsive gambling, or switching sexual addiction for workaholism.

Many recovering people have said something to the effect of, ''During periods of abstinence, I had a feeling of some kind of void inside of me. I had no idea what that was all about. Now I know that that was an empty space where God belonged.''

Why is it that a person can easily identify that food satisfies hunger and that water satisfies thirst, but does not as readily identify spiritual cravings?

There is an answer theologians consider to be the core of what humankind is all about: A human being is not just another animal, differing only in degree of intelligence. Humans, as morally free beings, can choose whether to recognize their spirituality and their unique relationship with God.

CHAPTER NINETEEN

ADDICTOLOGIA AND RELAPSE

A recurrence of addictive thinking often *precedes* relapse into drinking or use of other chemicals. Distorted thinking can also *follow* relapse as a person attempts to return to a Twelve Step program.

Recovery is a growth process. Relapse is an interruption of the growth process. But it is *not* "going back to square one." Yet almost without exception, that is what the relapser is likely to think. After two years or twelve years of recovery, a person who relapses may feel back on rock bottom. This mistaken conclusion can negatively impact a person's recovery from a relapse. The correct conclusion, as the following story illustrates, is that relapse doesn't wipe out the gains we have made to that point.

Slippery Spots

One winter day I had a package to mail at the post office. My car battery was dead, and I had to walk eight blocks to the post office. I tried to watch for slippery spots on the sidewalk, but in spite of my caution, I slipped and fell hard. While I fortunately did not break any bones, I did feel a jolting pain.

I may or may not have uttered a few expletives at the person who should have shoveled the sidewalk more thoroughly. But I knew that whether the fall was due to the deceptive appearance of the sidewalk or to my negligence, I was not going to get to the post office unless I got up and walked, pain and all. As I limped on, I was even more alert for possible slippery spots that might bring about another fall.

In spite of my painful fall, I was two blocks closer to my destination than when I had started. The fall did not erase the progress I had made.

This is how we can view relapse. Regardless of its pain, relapse is not a regression back to square one. The progress a person has made up to the point of the relapse can't be denied. The addict who has relapsed must start from that point, but as with the icy slip, the person must be even more alert to those things that can cause relapse.

What to Expect When Re-Entering
A Twelve Step Program

Sometimes an addictive thinking distortion is involved in recovery from relapse. I have seen people become frustrated upon returning to AA, NA, or another Twelve Step program. They remember the wonderful feeling, the glow, and the warmth they experienced on entering the Twelve Step program the first time and are disappointed when they don't get this feeling on re-entry.

But there is only one first kiss. The experience can never be duplicated.

The initial feeling on entering the Twelve Step program is similar. You find others like yourself, and you are made to feel welcome and comfortable as you become part of the recovery population. The person returning to the program looking for this feeling will likely be frustrated and disappointed.

Cocaine addicts have told me that throughout their addiction they tried in vain to recapture the high of their first use, but they could never do it. Attempting to re-experience the first high of recovery is quite similar.

Remember this, for it is important: *Be realistic about relapse.* The growth in sobriety that preceded relapse is not lost, and a person can't expect the original experience in recovery the second time around. These are two facts addictologia often distorts.

CHAPTER TWENTY

ADMITTING ERRORS

Many chemically dependent people have great difficulty admitting they are wrong. They may disagree with this statement, asserting that they would not have the slightest difficulty admitting they were wrong, *if* that were ever to occur.

One of the features of addictive thinking is the person's perception of always being right. Many of the other traits prevalent in addictive thinking — denial, projection, rationalization, omnipotence — are brought into play to bolster the insistence that the person has always been right.

Being Human Means Making Errors

The way addicts explain and defend their behavior may sound perfectly logical. Each incident explained may at first seem reasonable. If we take the entire litany of the incidents into account, however, it becomes evident that if the addict were indeed error-free, how did things end up in such a horrible mess? Upon re-examination of the addict's account, the addictive thinking becomes evident. Addicts' logical-sounding explanations are often only ingenious rationalizations and projections.

The recovering person must learn not only that it is all right to be human, but that it is the greatest achievement of all to be a fine human being. But one must first be human, which means that one must err at some time or another.

One of the most effective ways to accept the statement, "Making a mistake is not the end of the world," is seeing other people, especially those an addict holds in high regard, make mistakes too. Anyone can serve as a model for this. An example comes from my own life.

Ill-Fated Reunion

I once had a young psychiatric patient who was hospitalized for an extended time. As he recovered, he was given passes to leave the hospital for several hours.

One Friday, the patient told me he wanted to attend a class reunion the next day and meet with his classmates before they left for the four corners of the earth. I saw no reason to deny this request. Before I left him, the patient said, "Please remember to write that pass order on the chart; otherwise, the nurses will not let me out." I promised to do so, and I promptly went to the nurses' station and wrote the order.

When I met the patient the following Monday, he greeted me with a tearful and angry outburst. "Why did you lie to me? Why did you tell me I could go and then not let me go? Some of these classmates are going away, and I will never see them again!"

I told the patient that I had no idea what he was talking about, because I had written the pass order as I had promised.

"Then your nurses lied to me," he cried. "They said there was no such order on the chart."

I then examined the patient's chart, and, much to my amazement, there was no order there. What happened to the order I remembered writing?

The mystery was solved when I subsequently discovered the order *on another patient's chart.* I had indeed written the order as I had promised, but the nurses were correct in telling the patient there was no order for a pass on his chart, as indeed there was not. It was on someone else's chart.

I took both charts to the patient's room and showed him what had happened. I apologized for my mistake that had deprived him of seeing his classmates, and I told him that there was nothing I could do to right this error. All I could do was apologize.

Something strange happened, because there was a significant and progressive improvement in this patient's condition after this incident. It later turned out that one of the patient's major hang-ups was perfectionism. Making a mistake was taboo. He was obsessed with perfectionism and terrified of making a mistake.

But look here! His doctor made a mistake! And it was not just *any* kind of a mistake. A pass order written on the wrong chart could have conceivably resulted in a high-risk suicidal patient being permitted to leave the hospital. A doctor's mistake can be fatal, yet the doctor admitted it. Furthermore, the doctor continued to function as a doctor, the nurses still respected him, his orders were still being followed, even though he had made a mistake! Ergo, mistakes do not demolish a person. Maybe he, the patient, doesn't have to be eternally on guard to avoid a mistake.

CHAPTER TWENTY-ONE

THE FRUSTRATIONS OF GROWTH

Frustration is not the cause of alcoholism or other drug addiction. Many people have learned to tolerate frustration and somehow manage without escaping into the anesthesia of chemicals. People who do use chemicals to manage may have not learned how to tolerate frustration well. Perhaps they can manage some frustrations, but in their addictive thinking have great difficulty with others.

We become frustrated when we feel that things could and should be different than they are. When we know things are happening as could be expected, we do not become frustrated, even if we do not particularly like what is happening.

Life Is a Series of Challenges

What addictive thinkers often don't realize is that life is a series of ongoing challenges. We may put forth a great deal of effort to overcome one hurdle. No sooner do we begin to relax than we find ourselves confronting another hurdle, and this goes on ad infinitum.

Addictive thinkers may believe that there is something unusual about this. If they find themselves unable to go an extended period without some disturbance of their peace, they feel singled out and unjustly harassed. If they drink or use other chemicals, they will point to an intolerable series of problems with which they must try to cope. *It's just one thing after another,* they tell themselves. *Never a moment of peace.*

Although a legitimate complaint, this happens to be reality for most people. The addict is not apt to be aware of this. The way the addict sees it, no one else could possibly be subject to such terrible stresses and problems.

Persons close to the addict might know enough not to believe that the person has a legitimate excuse to use alcohol or other drugs. But they could be inadvertently lured into unhealthy empathy. The various problems the addict describes may sound like too much for anyone to bear. Upon closer analysis, though, an addict's problems are not that different from the non-addict's problems. But the addictive thinker's perception is that they are radically different: *Other people get a break once in a while, but not me. Never.*

Recovering addicts may bring their unrealistic expectations into sobriety. They may believe that other people in recovery have had an easier time. *My problems are the worst,* they think. *My spouse used to complain when I drank, and now I hear about my going to meetings every night. The supervisor watches me like a hawk. My old friends don't call anymore. . . .* As recovering people come into regular contact with others in recovery, however, they begin to see that everyone else doesn't have it better and, in fact, are a lot like they are.

Every aspect of recovery is subject to growth. Accepting life on its own terms, accepting powerlessness, surrendering to a Higher Power, taking and sharing a moral inventory, making amends — all these take place gradually. A person who has been recovering for several years may look back on early recovery and see how much there was to learn, how far he or she has come.

"Growing Pains"

A recovering alcoholic woman complained to me about the constant frustrations and crises she faced. As we examined them, it turned out that each crisis was making new demands on her. These additional demands were being made because she was doing well at her current level — each crisis was a take-off point for further growth.

"But this is so painful," she complained.

"Of course," I responded. "Haven't you ever heard of growing pains?"

"Well, how long do I have to keep growing?"

"We should all keep growing until we die," I said.

The Treatment Program Is Only the Beginning

Many people naively believe that they have completed their course in recovery when they "graduate" from a treatment program. At that point, it is difficult for them to understand that they have not yet even *begun* recovery. The treatment program is only an introduction; recovery is yet to come.

One of the worst things that can happen to a person who emerges from a treatment program is for everything to run smoothly for several weeks. This reinforces the fantasy that life can be devoid of challenges. The person begins to think how easy recovery is because those vexing problems are no longer occurring. When inevitable problems do occur, the person is caught off guard.

I tell the residents at our rehabilitation center that if they encounter difficulties in the first few weeks after discharge, they can blame me. I pray that they should not have things going too smoothly for the first few weeks because I want recovering addicts to encounter real life and experience the pressures of reality immediately. I want them to promptly use the tools they have been given during treatment:

- to call their sponsor,
- to attend meetings,
- to share with others, and
- to follow other recommendations.

Addictive thinkers may think they deserve to rest after their strenuous effort in treatment, but this kind of thinking can lead to relapse. Hurdles in the path are inevitable, and it is realistic to expect them in recovery.

CHAPTER TWENTY-TWO

ADDICTIVE THINKING
AND CODEPENDENCY

_____

If anyone were to think that addictologia is the only result of the effect of chemicals on brain function, the phenomenon of codependency effectively disproves this. We are all affected by other people's behavior in one way or another. Who is codependent? Various definitions and descriptions of codependency exist, but the one that seems most comprehensive is Melody Beattie's. *A codependent person is one who has let another person's behavior affect him or her, and who is obsessed with controlling that person's behavior.**

The important parts of this definition are the words *obsessed* and *controlling*. Obsessive thoughts crowd out all other thoughts, and they drain mental energy. Obsessive thoughts may intrude at any time, and, strangely enough, any attempt to get rid of obsessive thoughts may only increase their intensity.

_____

*Melody Beattie, *Codependent No More* (Center City, Minn.: Hazelden Educational Materials, 1987), 31.

Trying to drive away obsessive thoughts is like trying to get a coiled spring out of the way by compressing it. The more pressure that is exerted against the spring, the harder it recoils.

At the risk of oversimplification, we might say that the addicted person is *plagued* by a compulsion: the compulsion to use chemicals. A codependent person is *obsessed* by the addict's use and by the need to control.

Obsessions and compulsions are closely related. The term *obsessive-compulsive neurosis* has been used in psychiatry for many years. Both obsession and compulsion are characterized by the person's being preoccupied, and even consumed, by something irrational. In an *obsessional neurosis*, it is an irrational idea that plagues the person. In a *compulsive neurosis*, it is an irrational *act*. The reason the two are joined in psychiatry is that in almost every instance where the person is obsessed with an idea, there is some compulsive behavior. In virtually every case of compulsive behavior, there are obsessional thoughts. The following story illustrates how obsessional thoughts work.

The Chair on the Desk

While teaching psychiatry to medical students, I had a student who expressed interest in learning more about hypnosis. I felt that the most effective method of teaching this was to hypnotize him and allow him to learn firsthand what a hypnotic trance is and the various phenomena that can be produced under hypnosis.

This young man happened to be an excellent hypnotic subject, and in several sessions, I was able to demonstrate the various applications of hypnosis. Inasmuch as I also wanted him to understand the phenomenon of post-hypnotic suggestion, I said the following to him:

"Some time after you emerge from this trance, I will give you a signal, consisting of my picking up my pencil and tapping it on the desk. At that point, you will get up, pick up the chair on which you are sitting, and place it on my desk. However, you will have no memory that I gave this instruction." I then brought him out of the trance, and we continued our discussion about hypnosis.

After several moments, I nonchalantly picked up my pencil and tapped it lightly on the desk, while continuing the conversation. Within a few moments, the student, obviously uncomfortable, began to fidget. "I have this crazy urge to pick up my chair and put it on your desk," he said.

"Why should you want to do that?" I asked.

"I don't know. It's a crazy idea, but I just feel like I have to do it." He paused. "Did you tell me something like that during the trance?"

"Yes, I did."

"Then why can't I remember it?" he asked.

"Because when I gave you the suggestion, I told you that you would not remember it."

"Then I don't have to do it, do I?"

"I guess not," I answered.

Shortly afterward, we terminated the session and the student left. About twenty minutes later, the door flew open, the student burst into my office, picked up the chair, and angrily placed it on the desk. "Damn you!" he said, and turned around and left in a fury.

This is the nature of an obsession or compulsion, whether it occurs from a suggestion given under hypnosis or from a subconscious urge from some unknown origin. Just as putting a chair on a desk is nonsensical, a compulsive act can be irrational, yet the urge to do it may be virtually irresistible. Trying to resist the urge can produce so much anxiety and discomfort that the individual may give in to it simply to get relief from the intense pressure. With most obsessions and compulsions, this period of relief is quite brief; then the urge recurs, often with even greater force than previously.

Codependent people often behave in these obsessive-compulsive ways when they try to control an addict's behavior or use of chemicals. They may be obsessed with "trying to help" the addict, or later, if their efforts have failed, with punishing the addict.

The function of these and the many other psychological defenses that operate within us is often to preserve our *status quo;* that is, to allow us to continue doing what we are doing while trying to minimize the stress of our behavior. The most common of these defenses are *rationalization* and *projection*, which serve to make irrational things seem less irrational. For example, "There is nothing wrong with my job performance, and I am not an alcoholic. This is nothing but character assasination by those who are envious of my position." Other examples of rationalization and projection are:

- The person who refuses to go to AA, and says, "I went to some meetings and I saw some people leave the meeting and go right to a bar." He paid no attention to 98 percent of people who did not go to a bar. Instead of going to a meeting where 98 percent of those present do *not* drink, he goes to a bar where 100 percent of the people *do* drink.
- The overeater who says, "I can take a dessert [actually pigging out] because I skipped breakfast and had only lettuce and cottage cheese for lunch."
- The addict who says, "The reason I keep some cocaine in the house is because as long as it is there and I don't use it, I know I am cured."

How Addiction and Codependency Are Similar

Similarities between the behavior of an addict and the behavior of a codependent are striking. Addicts are usually looking for new ways to continue to use chemicals while trying to avoid their destructive consequences. A person might drink alcohol or use cocaine ''only on weekends'' or get a measured amount that will give the desired ''high'' but not enough to result in intoxication. When the efforts at control fail, addicts do not conclude, *I can't control my use.* Instead, they tell themselves, *That method did not work. I must find another method that does work.*

In the same way, codependents will not conclude that since efforts to stop the addict have been futile, there is no controlling the addict. Rather, they look for new ways that will work.

Remember the comment of the man who said, ''I am now *absolutely certain* that I cannot stop on my own, *maybe*''? It demonstrates how the addict can think in ways that are self-contradictory, yet feel they make perfectly good sense. The same is true in codependency. The following stories illustrate this point.

"I Could Never Go to Al-Anon"

The wife of a surgeon consulted me because of her husband's alcoholism. ''His drinking has progressively increased. He now comes home from work, sits down in front of the television with his supply of beer, and that's where he wakes up the next morning. So far he has been able to make it to the hospital every morning, but it's inevitable that before too long he'll not be able to show up for surgery, or he'll come into the operating room intoxicated, and it will all be out in the open. He's going to lose his hospital privileges before long.''

The woman stated that during the past few years their home life had deteriorated due to the alcoholism. Father and son were no longer talking to each other. The couple had no social life. They no longer had sexual relations.

The surgeon's wife had put up with all the consequences of the alcoholism until now. Since he was on the verge of ruining his career and livelihood, she felt she had to do something.

She had tried to talk to him numerous times about this, but he refused suggestions for help, believing he had no problem with alcohol. He told her that if she didn't like it, she could leave.

Since neither she nor the son appeared to have any leverage, there was no point in confronting him. The wife believed that if he were confronted, he would continue to refuse help, and he would tell them to leave the house.

Because there did not appear to be any effective approach toward the husband, I suggested the woman begin looking after her own needs and start attending Al-Anon meetings. I also arranged a meeting with another physician, a surgeon who was now in successful recovery and whose history had been almost identical to her husband's.

At this meeting, the recovering surgeon described how all of his wife's efforts to get him to quit had been futile, how he had continued drinking until his alcoholism became obvious at work. After his hospital privileges were suspended, he had come into treatment — but only under coercion and with the promise that if he successfully completed treatment, he would have his privileges restored. He had had a rocky course until he finally stabilized in sobriety.

"My wife is now in Al-Anon," he said. "Perhaps if she had been in Al-Anon earlier, I might have come to my senses without having lost my staff privileges, and my recovery could have been a smoother one. I suggest you start going to Al-Anon now, and my wife will be only too happy to take you to your first meeting, even tonight."

The woman shook her head. "Oh, no," she said. "I could never go to Al-Anon."

"Why not?" we asked.

"Because what would happen if someone recognized me and came to the conclusion that my husband was an alcoholic? Why, the word would get around, and my husband would lose all his patients. Who would allow themselves to be operated on by an alcoholic?''

I was baffled by her remark. ''I don't understand something,'' I said. ''You stated that you had put up with all of the problems that the alcoholism was causing. The only reason you consulted me was because you felt that exposure was imminent, that any day now he would walk into the operating room obviously intoxicated, and this would result in his suspension. Since this appears imminent, why are you reluctant to go to Al-Anon? From what you said, he is going to hit bottom in a much more serious way if the alcoholism is not arrested. From what this doctor is saying, his opinion is that his wife's participation in Al-Anon could actually have forestalled that happening to him.''

Regardless of what we both said, the woman held her ground. She could not go to Al-Anon because she felt that would expose the problem. She couldn't see that Al-Anon was the only thing that she could do that might help her avoid the disastrous consequences she feared.

"I Have Nothing in Common with Them"

In another case, the husband of an executive who had relapsed after detoxification called for help. He stated that his wife refused to attend Alcoholics Anonymous. After leaving the hospital, she had gone to several meetings, but she believed that the meetings were not for her. She was different than the other people at the meetings; she believed she had nothing in common with them.

I told the husband that his wife's resistance to AA was not unusual. After all, in AA she would learn that she could not drink again, and this was something that she did not want to hear.

''How are you doing with your Al-Anon program?'' I asked.

''I am not going to Al-Anon,'' he said. ''I went to two meetings, but that program is not for me. I have nothing in common with the people there.''

I pointed out to the man that he was parroting his wife's exact words. Although he criticized her for not participating in a recovery program and for feeling that she was different than the other alcoholics, he avoided his own recovery program for the same reason.

The anxiety about change can be so intense that people, like those in our examples, contradict themselves.

Making Changes

How is it that a person can be so blatantly self-contradictory, yet be unable to recognize this even if it is pointed out? In one word, the answer is *denial*. Much of the denial in addictive, distorted thinking is due to intense resistance to change. As long as a person can deny reality, he or she can continue behaving the same as before. Acceptance of reality might commit him or her to the very difficult process of change.

Often, people have no problem with changes as long as the change occurs in someone else.

An Experiment: The Difficulty of Making Changes

Just for fun, try the following experiment: Fold your hands across your chest, and then observe the position of your hands. Some people fold the left hand over the right, and others do the reverse.

After noting how you do it, unfold your hands. Now fold them again, but this time in the opposite way; that is, if you normally put your right hand over your left, put your left hand over your right.

You will probably notice how awkward this feels. The old way is normal and relaxing. The new way may seem strange, and you may feel you could never relax in this position.

If a simple change in position of your hands is so uncomfortable, just think how uncomfortable it is to change part of your behavior or lifestyle.

Codependents may eagerly seek help, thinking experts can tell them what to do to stop someone from using chemicals. They are disappointed when they learn that they can do nothing to alter the addict's behavior, that they are powerless. When the expert suggests that they look at their own behavior and begin to make changes in themselves, they likely will back away. They are particularly apt to be turned off when people in Al-Anon tell them, "We don't come here to change our spouse. We come here to change ourselves."

"Change myself?" they may respond. "Why should I change myself? I'm not the one who's drinking!"

Distorted Perceptions

Two contradictory ideas cannot coexist in normal logic. But they can exist in addictologia. This is not a criticism of people who are codependent. Codependents are people who are suffering, often intensely. They are extremely sensitive. Whatever we say to describe the addictive thinking of either an addict or a codependent is not meant to be pejorative.

Many of the features of addictologia in the addict have their counterpart in a codependent because they are from a similar origin: a sense of low self-esteem.

I believe that most emotional problems that are not of physical origin are due, in one way or another, to low self-esteem. By low self-esteem, I mean negative feelings people have about themselves that are not justified by fact. In other words, some people have a distorted self-perception, but in contrast to people who have grandiose delusions about themselves, people with low self-esteem have delusions of inferiority, incompetence, and worthlessness. Strangely enough, these feelings of inadequacy are often particularly intense in people who are the most gifted.

115

If our perceptions of ourselves are incorrect, we will probably be prone to maladjustments in our life as well. We can only adjust to reality if we have an accurate perception of it.

The Rule of the Three C's

In Al-Anon there is a rule of the Three C's: you did not CAUSE it, you cannot CONTROL it, and you cannot CURE it. But many people do feel responsible for another's addiction, do try to control it, and do believe that they can cure it.

Sometimes it seems as though the codependent person is thinking, *I am so powerful that I can cause addiction, or control it, or cure it.* This isn't really a feeling of superiority or arrogance. Quite the contrary, such feelings are often a defensive reaction against feelings of inferiority.

Often, the Three C's are related to openly acknowledged inferiority. For example, the codependent person thinks, *I am the cause of my daughter's addiction because if I had been a better parent, she would have not turned to drugs. If I had provided her with the love and support she needed, she would not have sought chemicals. The addiction is due to my dereliction. If only I were a better person, she would use less or quit.* These feelings are particularly common for the codependent when the other person is in the early phases of addiction.

Other Beliefs Codependent People Often Have

Beyond the three C's, low self-esteem contributes to other beliefs codependent people usually have. Codependents often

- don't trust their own judgment, and they accept the addict's view of the world as correct.
- feel obligated to justify their existence by caring for others, sometimes accepting martyrdom as deserved.
- believe that they are tied to the addict because they feel they lack the personal resources to make it on their own.

- find it easy to believe derogatory comments that the addict makes about them.
- resist doing the best they can for themselves because they don't believe they deserve the best.
- think of themselves as unlovable.
- are afraid to feel or express anger because they do not trust themselves to maintain control over it.
- think if they are angry, others will reject them.

In summary, addictive thinking and codependency have much in common. In both, there is often denial, rationalization, and projection. In both, contradictory ideas can coexist, and there is fierce resistance to change oneself and a desire to change others. In both, there is a delusion of control, and in both there is invariably low self-esteem. Thus, all the features of addictologia are present in both, and the only distinguishing feature may be the use or non-use of a chemical.

CHAPTER TWENTY-THREE

RIDICULOUS EXPLANATIONS, SENSIBLE SOLUTIONS

When we see addictive people behave irrationally, we are often so stunned that we don't know how to react. We are much like the farmer who for the first time in his life sees a giraffe in the zoo and says, "I see it, but I don't believe it." *It is obvious that what addicts are doing is destructive to themselves and others*, the person thinks, *so why aren't addicts able to relate their behavior to alcohol and other chemicals?*

When a psychotic person behaves insanely, it does not cause us to lose our bearings. But when a person who is otherwise perfectly sane and rational does crazy things, we are taken aback. We may begin to doubt our senses, asking ourselves, *Could it be that what I see is really happening?* This self-doubt may be so intense that we are vulnerable to accept the most ridiculous explanations as being sensible!

The addictive person's thinking processes may be so affected by the action of chemicals on the brain that the wildest self-contradictions and inconsistencies in behavior are understandable. Indeed, when addicted people recover and look back at the irrational behavior, they are frequently amazed at how they thought and acted. What is less understandable is how and why the significant others in the addict's environment, whose minds are unaltered by chemicals, fall prey to so much distorted thought and behavior.

The answer is that all of us have unique needs, some healthy, some not so healthy, and the emotional pressure to gratify these needs can greatly affect the way we think and feel. Sometimes these emotional pressures can distort our thinking almost or just as much as the chemical used by the addict.

This is why the concept of addictologia is so important to understand. Addictive thinking exists and is operative in every addicted person, and, to a greater or lesser degree, in the significant others.

Testing Reality

In ordinary life, no one stops to ask, *Is it possible that I am hallucinating?* We cannot function well in reality if we doubt everything. When the bus arrives at the bus stop, we get on the bus and do not think, *Maybe this bus does not really exist. Maybe I'm just hallucinating a bus.* Such thinking would paralyze us.

When things occur that are totally beyond our expectations, we may pinch ourselves to be sure that we are not dreaming. This can occur when anything out of the ordinary happens, whether it is something good or terrible. We pinch ourselves to test reality.

It may be asking too much of active addicts to try to discover whether their perceptions are real or distorted. But people whose brains are unaffected by chemicals and who relate to a chemical user would be wise to check out their own thinking, as well as put the addict's behavior in proper perspective. This holds true whether we are a husband, wife, parent, child, therapist, employer, friend, pastor, or anyone else relating to an active addict. The more we understand how addicts think and function, the less likely we are to be paralyzed by the shock of their behavior, and the less likely we are to be taken in by their ingenious cunning and deviousness. Furthermore, if we can grasp that there are powerful forces within ourselves that are capable of producing many of the same distortions that result from chemicals, we may be less resistant when our role as codependents is pointed out to us.

Two Plus Two Equals Five

The mother of the young man who was destroying himself with alcohol and other drugs could not understand how he could be oblivious to the disastrous effects that chemicals were having on his life. She asked for help in dealing with him. "But don't tell me I have to put him out of the house or that I should not bail him out of jail," she said. "I don't want to hear that."

My response was, "Please tell me how much is two plus two, but don't say four." She had been unable to see that her own thinking was no less distorted than her son's. Why was her thinking distorted? Because when she bailed him out of jail or didn't put him out of the house, she enabled him to go on using chemicals without seeing the magnitude of the problem. She kept him from his rock-bottom experience from which recovery would be possible.

How to Clarify Your Own Reality

Addictologia is a new word, not a new concept. If you read the literature on addiction, addictive thinking will jump out at you from every page. The value in giving it a name is precisely to make it more recognizable and to understand its crucial role in addiction.

Is severe pain normal? No. Is it normal for a person with a fractured leg to be in severe pain? Yes.

Is fever normal? No. Is it normal for a person with an infection to have a high fever? Yes.

Is addictologia normal? No. Is it normal for chemically dependent people and codependents to have addictologia? Yes.

Since you are reading this book, you are, in one way or another, concerned about addiction. As such, you can be vulnerable to addictive thinking. Check this out with someone who can take a more objective look at your life. With the help of another, you will be more able to clarify your own reality.

SELECT BIBLIOGRAPHY

Beattie, Melody. *Codependent No More*. Center City, Minn.: Hazelden Educational Materials, 1987.

Lindquist, Marie. *Holding Back: Why We Hide the Truth About Ourselves*. Center City, Minn.: Hazelden Educational Materials, 1987.

One Day at a Time in Al-Anon. New York: Al-Anon Family Group Headquarters, 1986.

Rosellini, Gayle, and Mark Worden. *Of Course You're Angry*. Center City, Minn.: Hazelden Educational Materials, 1987.

Sedlak, David, M.D. *Childhood: Setting the Stage for Addiction in Childhood and Adolescence*. Richard Isralowitz and Mark Singer, eds. New York: Haworth Press, 1983.

Twelve Steps and Twelve Traditions. 38th ed. New York: Alcoholics Anonymous World Services, Inc., 1988.

Twenty-Four Hours a Day. rev. ed. Center City, Minn.: Hazelden Educational Materials, 1975.

Twerski, Abraham J., M.D. *Like Yourself: And Others Will Too*. Englewood Cliffs, N.J.: Prentice Hall, 1978.

_____. *Self-Discovery in Recovery*. Center City, Minn.: Hazelden Educational Materials, 1984.

_____. *Caution: Kindness Can Be Dangerous to the Alcoholic*. Englewood Cliffs, N.J.: Prentice Hall, 1981.